Pasta & Bakes

Pasta &
Bakes

Cooking Your Way to Good Living

PaRragon

Bath • New York • Cologne • Melbourne • Delhi
Hong Kong • Shenzhen • Singapore

This edition published by Parragon Books Ltd in 2016
LOVE FOOD is an imprint of Parragon Books Ltd

Parragon Books Ltd
Chartist House
15–17 Trim Street
Bath BA1 1HA, UK
www.parragon.com/lovefood

ISBN 978-1-4748-4996-8

Printed in China

Internal design by Ignition
Additional photography by Mike Cooper
Additional food styling by Lincoln Jefferson

Notes for the Reader

- This book uses both metric and imperial measurements. Follow the same units of measurement throughout; do not mix metric and imperial. All spoon measurements are level: teaspoons are assumed to be 5 ml, and tablespoons are assumed to be 15 ml. Unless otherwise stated, milk is assumed to be full fat, eggs and individual fruits and vegetables are medium, pepper is freshly ground black pepper and salt is table salt. A pinch of salt is calculated as $\frac{1}{16}$ of a teaspoon. Unless otherwise stated, all root vegetables should be peeled prior to using.

- The times given are an approximate guide only. Preparation times differ according to the techniques used by different people and the cooking times may also vary from those given.

- For best results, use a food thermometer when cooking meat. Check the latest government guidelines for current advice.

Pasta is arguably the most useful ingredient to be found in any kitchen. It goes with just about anything else you can think of – from vegetables and cheese to meat and fish. It's equally delicious served with simple, inexpensive sauces or extravagant and luxurious mixtures; it can be added to soups or form the basis of filling baked dishes. It may be a main meal, a starter or a delightfully different salad.

Pasta is very versatile so it's easy to find fabulous recipes for all occasions and every season of the year. Virtually everyone loves pasta and it's especially popular with children. High in complex carbohydrates, it provides a steady release of energy but contains hardly any fat. Depending on the type of wheat flour used in its manufacture, it can also be a good source of protein, as well as B vitamins, potassium and iron. Moreover, it's economical, convenient and the dried variety keeps well. Huge numbers of pasta dishes can be prepared and cooked within 30 minutes and many take only half that time.

There are hundreds of pasta shapes and new ones are being introduced all the time. There are no hard and fast rules about which shape goes with a particular sauce, although there are some traditional partnerships, such as Spaghetti Bolognese and Fettucine all'Alfredo. However, there are some useful guidelines.

Long, thin pasta, such as spaghetti and linguine, is ideal for seafood sauces and light olive oil or fresh tomato dressings, but cannot really hold thick or chunky sauces. These are better served with pasta shapes that trap the sauce in hollows and ridges – penne (quills), fusilli (spirals) or conchiglie (shells), for example. Flat ribbons, such as tagliatelle, fettucine and pappardelle, are perfect for rich or creamy sauces.

Baked dishes are often made with lasagne (flat sheets of pasta that can be layered with a variety of sauces) or cannelloni (tubes that can be filled and baked in a sauce). Smaller shapes, such as macaroni and rigatoni, are also often used in baking.

Very small pasta shapes, such as stellete (stars) and anellini (rings), are used in soups, and filled pasta, such as ravioli and tortellini, is also often served in broth.

MAKING FRESH PASTA

If you want to make filled pasta, such as tortellini, you will need to prepare the dough yourself. The same basic dough can also be used to make lasagne sheets and a variety of shapes, such as tagliatelle, pappardelle and macaroni. You need no special equipment and the process is both easy and satisfying.

Basic Pasta Dough
Serves 3–4
Preparation time: 15 minutes, plus 30 minutes resting

200 g/7 oz strong white flour, plus extra for dusting
pinch of salt
2 eggs, lightly beaten
1 tbsp olive oil

1 Sift together the flour and salt onto a work surface and make a well in the centre with your fingers. Pour the eggs and oil into the well then, using the fingers of one hand, gradually incorporate the flour into the liquid.
2 Knead the dough on a lightly floured work surface until it is completely smooth. Wrap in clingfilm and leave to rest for 30 minutes before rolling out or feeding through a pasta machine. Resting makes the dough more elastic.

FLAVOURED PASTA

Basic pasta dough may be flavoured and coloured by the addition of other ingredients.

Tomato pasta: Add 2 tbsp tomato purée to the well in the flour and use only 1½ eggs instead of 2.

Spinach pasta: Blanch 225 g/8 oz spinach in boiling water for 1 minute, then drain and squeeze out as much liquid as possible. Alternatively, use 150 g/5½ oz thawed frozen spinach. This does not need blanching, but as much liquid as possible should be squeezed out. Finely chop the spinach and mix with the flour before making a well and adding the eggs and oil.

Herb pasta: Add 3 tbsp finely chopped fresh herbs to the flour before making a well and adding the eggs and oil.

Saffron pasta: Soak a sachet of powdered saffron in 2 tbsp hot water for 15 minutes. Use 1½ eggs and whisk the saffron water into them.

Wholemeal pasta: Use 140 g/5 oz wholemeal flour and 25 g/1 oz strong white flour.

ROLLING OUT PASTA DOUGH

When the fresh dough has rested, it may be rolled out by hand or with a pasta machine. Larger quantities of dough should be halved or cut into thirds before rolling out. Keep covered until you are ready to work on them.

To roll out by hand, lightly dust a work surface with plain flour, then roll out the pasta dough with a lightly floured rolling pin, always rolling away from you and turning the dough a quarter turn each time. Keep rolling to make a rectangle 2–3 mm/ ¹⁄₁₆–⅛ inch thick. The dough can then be cut into ribbons, stamped out with a biscuit cutter or cut into squares to make ravioli.

A pasta machine makes rolling out the dough easier and quicker and ensures that it is even. There are a number of models available, the most useful being a hand-cranked machine with attachable cutters. An electric machine is even easier to use but somewhat extravagant.

Cut the dough into manageable size pieces – 1 quantity Basic Pasta Dough should be cut into 4 pieces, for example. Flatten a piece with your hand and wrap the others in clingfilm until required. Fold the flat piece into thirds and feed it through the pasta machine on its widest setting. Repeat the folding and rolling 3 or 4 more times on this setting, then close the rollers by one notch. Continue feeding the dough through the rollers, without folding into thirds, gradually reducing the setting until you reach the narrowest. If you want to make ribbons, cut the dough into 30-cm/12-inch strips and feed through the appropriate cutter.

CUTTING AND SHAPING FRESH PASTA

Pasta machines usually have a wide cutter for tagliatelle and a narrower one for tagliarini. Other pasta shapes can be cut by hand, as can hand-rolled pasta dough.

To make pappardelle, use a serrated pasta wheel to cut 2.5 cm/1 inch wide ribbons from the rolled-out dough. To make tagliatelle or tagliarini, roll up a strip of dough like a Swiss roll and then cut into 5-mm/ ¼-inch slices (tagliatelle) or 3-mm/⅛-inch slices (tagliarini) with a sharp knife. To make macaroni, cut the pasta dough into 2.5-cm/1-inch squares with a sharp knife, then roll them corner to corner around a chopstick to form tubes. Slide off and leave to dry slightly.

Italians use the word ravioli as an all-purpose term for filled pasta and it can, therefore, be a variety of shapes.

Soups & Salads

SERVES 4

2 tbsp olive oil
2 garlic cloves, chopped
2 red onions, chopped
75 g/2¾ oz Parma ham, sliced
1 red pepper, deseeded and chopped
1 orange pepper, deseeded and chopped

400 g/14 oz canned chopped tomatoes
1 litre/1¾ pints vegetable stock
1 celery stick, chopped
400 g/14 oz canned borlotti beans
100 g/3½ oz green leafy cabbage, shredded

75 g/2¾ oz frozen peas, defrosted
1 tbsp chopped fresh parsley
75 g/2¾ oz dried vermicelli
salt and pepper
freshly grated Parmesan cheese, to serve

Minestrone

Heat the oil in a large saucepan. Add the garlic, onions and Parma ham and cook over a medium heat, stirring, for 3 minutes, until slightly softened. Add the red and orange peppers and the chopped tomatoes and cook for a further 2 minutes, stirring. Stir in the stock, then add the celery. Drain and add the borlotti beans along with the cabbage, peas and parsley. Season to taste with salt and pepper. Bring to the boil, then lower the heat and simmer for 30 minutes.

Add the vermicelli to the pan. Cook for a further 10–12 minutes, or according to the instructions on the packet. Remove from the heat and ladle into serving bowls. Sprinkle with freshly grated Parmesan cheese and serve immediately.

SERVES 4

2 tomatoes, chopped
1 garlic clove, chopped
¼ onion, chopped
1 tbsp vegetable oil
1.2 litres/2 pints chicken or vegetable stock
115 g/4 oz vermicelli, broken into short lengths

¼–½ fresh red chilli, deseeded and finely sliced
115 g/4 oz baby kale or spinach, tough stems removed, leaves sliced into ribbons
3 tbsp chopped fresh coriander

60 g/2¼ oz feta cheese, diced
4 tbsp soured cream
salt and pepper
finely diced red onion, to garnish

Mexican vermicelli Soup

Put the tomatoes, garlic and onion in a blender and purée until smooth. Heat a small frying pan, add the oil and fry the purée over medium heat for about 5 minutes, until slightly reduced.

Bring the stock to the boil in a large saucepan. Add the vermicelli and cook for 5 minutes, then add the chilli, kale and the reduced purée. Season to taste with salt and pepper. Cover and simmer over a medium-low heat for 6–8 minutes, until the vermicelli is tender. Stir in 2 tablespoons of the coriander.

Put the cheese in the bottom of individual bowls, then ladle the soup over the top. Add a tablespoon of soured cream to each bowl, and sprinkle with red onion and the remaining coriander. Serve immediately.

SERVES 6

300 g/10½ oz canned cannellini beans, drained and rinsed
300 g/10½ oz canned borlotti beans, drained and rinsed

about 600 ml/1 pint chicken or vegetable stock
115 g/4 oz dried conchigliette
4–5 tbsp olive oil

2 garlic cloves, very finely chopped
3 tbsp chopped fresh flat-leaf parsley
salt and pepper

Tuscan Bean Soup

Place half the cannellini beans and half the borlotti beans in a food processor with half the stock and process until smooth. Pour into a large heavy-based saucepan and add the remaining beans. Stir in enough of the remaining stock to achieve the consistency you like, then bring to the boil.

Add the pasta and return to the boil, then reduce the heat and cook for 15 minutes, or until just tender.

Meanwhile, heat 3 tablespoons of the oil in a small frying pan. Add the garlic and cook, stirring constantly, for 2–3 minutes, or until golden. Stir the garlic into the soup with the parsley.

Season to taste with salt and pepper and ladle into warmed soup bowls. Drizzle with the remaining oil to taste and serve immediately.

SERVES 4

2 tbsp olive oil
3 rashers rindless, smoked bacon, finely chopped
25 g/1 oz butter
450 g/1 lb floury potatoes, chopped

450 g/1 lb onions, finely chopped
600 ml/1 pint chicken stock
600 ml/1 pint milk
100 g/3½ oz dried conchigliette

150 ml/5 fl oz double cream
2 tbsp chopped parsley
2 tbsp green pesto
salt and pepper
freshly grated Parmesan cheese, to serve

Potato & Pesto Soup

Heat the oil in a large saucepan and cook the bacon over a medium heat for 4 minutes. Add the butter, potatoes and onions and cook for 12 minutes, stirring constantly.

Add the stock and milk to the saucepan, bring to the boil and simmer for 5 minutes. Add the conchigliette and simmer for a further 3–4 minutes.

Blend in the cream and simmer for 5 minutes. Add the parsley and pesto and season to taste with salt and pepper. Sprinkle with freshly grated Parmesan cheese and serve immediately.

SERVES 4

4 rashers streaky bacon, cut into small squares
1 onion, chopped
2 garlic cloves, crushed
2 celery sticks, chopped
50 g/1 ¾ oz dried farfalline
400 g/14 oz canned brown lentils, drained
1.2 litres/2 pints vegetable stock
2 tbsp chopped fresh mint, plus extra sprigs to garnish

Brown Lentil & Pasta Soup

Place the bacon in a large frying pan together with the onion, garlic and celery. Dry-fry for 4–5 minutes, stirring, until the onion is tender and the bacon is just beginning to brown.

Add the pasta to the frying pan and cook, stirring, for 1 minute to coat the pasta in the fat.

Add the lentils and the vegetable stock and bring to the boil. Reduce the heat and leave to simmer for 12–15 minutes, or until the pasta is tender but still firm to the bite.

Remove the frying pan from the heat and stir in the chopped fresh mint. Transfer the soup to warmed soup bowls, garnish with fresh mint sprigs and serve immediately.

SERVES 6

1 quantity Basic Pasta
   Dough (see p6)
1 egg white
2 litres/3½ pints chicken
   stock
2 tbsp finely chopped
   fresh tarragon leaves
freshly grated Parmesan
   cheese, to serve

filling
200 g/7 oz cooked
   chicken, roughly
   chopped
½ tsp grated lemon rind

2 tbsp chopped mixed
   fresh tarragon, chives
   and parsley
4 tbsp whipping cream
salt and pepper

Chicken Ravioli in Tarragon Broth

To make the filling, put the chicken, lemon rind and mixed herbs in a food
processor and season to taste with salt and pepper. Chop finely, by pulsing; do
not overprocess. Scrape into a bowl and stir in the cream. Taste and adjust the
seasoning, if necessary.

Divide the pasta dough in half. Cover one half and roll the other half on a floured
surface as thinly as possible, less than 1.5 mm/⅟₁₆ inch. Cut out rectangles
measuring about 10 x 5 cm/4 x 2 inches.

Place rounded teaspoons of filling on one half of the dough pieces. Brush around
the edges with egg white and fold in half. Press the edges gently but firmly to seal.
Arrange the ravioli in one layer on a baking sheet, dusted generously with flour.
Repeat with the remaining dough. Allow the ravioli to dry in a cool place for about
15 minutes or chill for 1–2 hours.

Bring a large saucepan of lightly salted water to the boil over a medium heat. Drop
in half the ravioli and cook for 12–15 minutes, until just tender. Drain on a clean tea
towel while cooking the remainder.

Meanwhile, put the stock and tarragon in a large saucepan. Bring to the boil and
reduce the heat to bubble very gently. Cover and simmer for about 15 minutes,
to infuse. Add the cooked ravioli and simmer for a further 5 minutes. Ladle into
warmed soup bowls to serve immediately, sprinkled with the Parmesan cheese.

SERVES 4

450 g/1 lb skinless, boneless chicken breasts, cut into thin strips
1.2 litres/2 pints chicken stock

150 ml/5 fl oz double cream
115 g/4 oz dried vermicelli
1 tbsp cornflour

3 tbsp milk
175 g/6 oz canned sweetcorn kernels, drained
salt and pepper

Italian Chicken Soup

Place the chicken in a large saucepan and pour in the chicken stock and cream. Bring to the boil, then reduce the heat and simmer for 20 minutes.

Meanwhile, bring a large saucepan of lightly salted water to the boil over a medium heat. Add the pasta, return to the boil and cook for 8–10 minutes, or until just tender but still firm to the bite. Drain the pasta well and keep warm.

Season the saucepan of chicken to taste with salt and pepper. Mix the cornflour and milk together until a smooth paste forms, then stir it into the soup. Add the sweetcorn and pasta and heat through. Ladle the soup into warmed soup bowls and serve immediately.

SERVES 6

1 tbsp olive oil
500 g/1 lb 2 oz fresh lean
   beef mince
2 onions, finely chopped
2 garlic cloves, finely
   chopped
2 tbsp plain flour
225 ml/8 fl oz water

400 g/14 oz canned
   chopped tomatoes
1 carrot, finely chopped
225 g/8 oz red pepper,
   roasted, peeled,
   deseeded and
   chopped
1 tsp Hungarian paprika
¼ tsp caraway seeds

pinch of dried oregano
1 litre/1¾ pints beef stock
55 g/2 oz tagliatelle,
   broken into small
   pieces
salt and pepper
soured cream and sprigs
   of fresh coriander,
   to garnish

Beef Goulash Soup

Heat the oil in a large wide saucepan over a medium-high heat. Add the beef and season to taste with salt and pepper. Fry until lightly browned. Reduce the heat and add the onions and garlic. Cook for about 3 minutes, stirring frequently, until the onions are softened. Stir in the flour and continue cooking for 1 minute.

Add the water and stir to combine well, scraping the bottom of the pan to mix in the flour. Stir in the tomatoes, carrot, red pepper, paprika, caraway seeds, oregano and stock. Bring just to the boil. Reduce the heat, cover and simmer gently for about 40 minutes, stirring occasionally, until all the vegetables are tender.

Add the tagliatelle to the soup and simmer for a further 20 minutes, or until the tagliatelle is cooked. Taste the soup and adjust the seasoning, if necessary. Ladle into warmed bowls and top each with a tablespoonful of soured cream. Garnish with coriander and serve.

SERVES 4

55 g/2 oz dried peas, soaked for 2 hours and drained

900 g/2 lb boned neck of veal, diced

1.2 litres/2 pints beef stock

600 ml/1 pint water

55 g/2 oz pearl barley, washed

1 large carrot, diced

1 small turnip (about 175 g/6 oz), diced

1 large leek, thinly sliced

1 red onion, finely chopped

100 g/3½ oz chopped tomatoes

1 fresh basil sprig

100 g/3½ oz dried vermicelli

salt and white pepper

Tuscan Veal Broth

Put the peas, veal, stock and water into a large pan and bring to the boil over a low heat. Using a slotted spoon, skim off any scum that rises to the surface.

When all of the scum has been removed, add the pearl barley and a pinch of salt to the mixture. Simmer gently over a low heat for 25 minutes.

Add the carrot, turnip, leek, onion, tomatoes and basil to the pan, and season to taste with salt and white pepper. Simmer for about 2 hours, skimming the surface from time to time to remove any scum. Remove the pan from the heat and set aside for 2 hours.

Set the pan over a medium heat and bring to the boil. Add the vermicelli and cook for 8–10 minutes, then remove and discard the basil. Ladle into soup bowls and serve immediately.

SERVES 6

2 tbsp olive oil
2 onions, sliced
1 garlic clove, finely
  chopped
1 litre/1¾ pints fish stock
  or water
400 g/14 oz canned
  chopped tomatoes

¼ tsp Herbes de Provence
¼ tsp saffron threads
115 g/4 oz dried
  macaroni
1 kg/2 lbs 4 oz live
  mussels, scrubbed and
  debearded

450 g/1 lb monkfish fillet,
  cut into chunks
225 g/8 oz raw prawns,
  peeled and deveined,
  tails left on
salt and pepper

Fish Soup with Macaroni

Heat the oil in a large heavy-based saucepan. Add the onions and garlic and cook over a low heat, stirring occasionally, for 5 minutes, or until the onions have softened.

Add the stock with the tomatoes and their can juices, herbs, saffron and pasta and season to taste with salt and pepper. Bring to the boil, then cover and simmer for 15 minutes.

Discard any mussels with broken shells or any that refuse to close when tapped. Add the mussels, monkfish and prawns to the saucepan. Re-cover the saucepan and simmer for a further 5–10 minutes, until the mussels have opened, the prawns have changed colour and the fish is opaque and flakes easily. Discard any mussels that remain closed. Ladle the soup into warmed bowls and serve.

SERVES 4

750 g/1 lb 10 oz mussels, scrubbed and debearded
2 tbsp olive oil
100 g/3½ oz butter
55 g/2 oz rindless streaky bacon, chopped

1 onion, chopped
2 garlic cloves, finely chopped
55 g/2 oz plain flour
3 potatoes, thinly sliced
115 g/4 oz dried farfalle

300 ml/10 fl oz double cream
1 tbsp lemon juice
2 egg yolks
salt and pepper
2 tbsp finely chopped fresh parsley, to garnish

Mussel & Pasta Soup

Discard any mussels with broken shells or any that refuse to close when tapped. Bring a large heavy-based saucepan of water to the boil. Add the mussels and oil and season to taste with pepper. Cover tightly and cook over a high heat for 5 minutes, or until the mussels have opened. Remove the mussels with a slotted spoon, discarding any that remain closed. Strain the cooking liquid through a muslin-lined sieve and reserve 1.2 litres/2 pints.

Melt the butter in a clean saucepan. Add the bacon, onion and garlic and cook over a low heat, stirring occasionally, for 5 minutes. Stir in the flour and cook, stirring, for 1 minute. Gradually stir in all but 2 tablespoons of the reserved cooking liquid and bring to the boil, stirring constantly. Add the potato slices and simmer for 5 minutes. Add the pasta and simmer for a further 10 minutes.

Stir in the cream and lemon juice and season to taste with salt and pepper. Add the mussels. Mix the egg yolks and the remaining mussel cooking liquid together, then stir the mixture into the soup and cook for 4 minutes, until thickened.

Ladle the soup into warmed soup bowls, garnish with chopped parsley and serve immediately.

SERVES 6

500 g/1 lb 2 oz shelled
   scallops
350 ml/12 fl oz milk
1.5 litres/2¾ pints basic
   vegetable stock
250 g/9 oz frozen petits
   pois

175 g/6 oz taglialini
70 g/2½ oz butter
2 spring onions, finely
   chopped
175 ml/6 fl oz dry white
   wine

3 slices of prosciutto, cut
   into thin strips
salt and pepper
chopped fresh parsley,
   to garnish

Quick Sea Scallop Soup with Pasta

Slice the scallops in half horizontally and season with salt and pepper.

Pour the milk and stock into a saucepan, add a pinch of salt and bring to the boil. Add the peas and pasta, bring back to the boil and cook for 8–10 minutes, until the taglialini is tender but still firm to the bite.

Meanwhile, melt the butter in a frying pan. Add the spring onions and cook over a low heat, stirring occasionally, for 3 minutes. Add the scallops and cook for 45 seconds on each side. Pour in the wine, add the prosciutto and cook for 2–3 minutes.

Stir the scallop mixture into the soup, taste and adjust the seasoning, if necessary, and garnish with parsley. Serve immediately.

SERVES 4

450 g/1 lb rump or sirloin steak in a single piece
450 g/1 lb dried fusilli
4 tbsp olive oil
2 tbsp lime juice

2 tbsp Thai fish sauce
2 tsp clear honey
4 spring onions, sliced
1 cucumber, peeled and cut into 2.5-cm/1-inch chunks

3 tomatoes, cut into wedges
1 tbsp finely chopped fresh mint
salt and pepper

Rare Roast Beef Pasta Salad

Season the steak with salt and pepper. Grill or pan-fry it for 4 minutes on each side. Allow to rest for 5 minutes, then slice thinly across the grain.

Meanwhile, bring a large saucepan of lightly salted water to the boil. Add the pasta, bring back to the boil and cook for 8–10 minutes, or until tender but still firm to the bite. Drain the fusilli, refresh in cold water and drain again thoroughly. Toss the fusilli in the olive oil and set aside until required.

Combine the lime juice, fish sauce and honey in a small saucepan and cook over a medium heat for 2 minutes.

Add the spring onions, cucumber, tomatoes and mint to the pan, then add the steak and mix well. Season to taste with salt and pepper.

Transfer the fusilli to a large, warmed serving dish and top with the steak and salad mixture. Serve just warm or allow to cool completely.

SERVES 4-6

115 g/4 oz egg pappardelle, broken into 7.5-cm/3-inch lengths
coarsely grated zest of 1 lemon

2 tbsp extra virgin olive oil
4 carrots
2 courgettes
125 g/4½ oz cooked chicken, sliced into thin strips

40 g/1½ oz walnut halves
5 tbsp snipped fresh chives
2 tsp white wine vinegar
3 tbsp walnut oil
salt and pepper

Chicken Pasta Salad with Walnuts

Bring a large saucepan of lightly salted water to the boil over a medium heat. Add the pasta and cook for 8–10 minutes, or until tender but still firm to the bite. Drain thoroughly and tip into a serving bowl. Toss with the lemon zest, 1 tablespoon of the olive oil and season to taste with salt and pepper.

Meanwhile, trim and peel the carrots. Slice lengthways into thin strips, using a mandolin or very sharp knife. Trim the courgettes and remove a wide band of peel on opposite sides. Slice lengthways into thin strips, so that there is a narrow strip of green peel on each side. Put the carrots in a steamer basket set over boiling water. Steam for 3 minutes, then add the courgettes. Steam for 2 minutes more until only just tender.

Add the vegetables, chicken, walnuts and chives to the pasta, tossing gently to mix. Whisk the vinegar with ½ teaspoon of salt and ¼ teaspoon of pepper. Whisk in the walnut oil and the remaining tablespoon of olive oil. Pour over the salad and toss again carefully. Leave to stand for 30 minutes to let the flavour develop. Serve at room temperature.

SERVES 4

125 g/4½ oz dried
  conchiglie
2 tbsp olive oil
1 medium onion,
  chopped
2 garlic cloves, very finely
  chopped

1 small yellow pepper,
  deseeded and cut into
  matchsticks
175 g/6 oz spicy pork
  sausage, such as
  chorizo, Italian
  pepperoni or salami,
  skinned and sliced

2 tbsp red wine
1 tbsp red wine vinegar
125 g/4½ oz mixed salad
  leaves
salt

Spicy Sausage Salad

Bring a large saucepan of lightly salted water to the boil over a medium heat. Add the pasta and cook for 8–10 minutes, or until tender but still firm to the bite. Drain thoroughly and reserve.

Heat the oil in a pan over a medium heat. Add the onion and cook until translucent. Stir in the garlic, yellow pepper and sausage and cook for about 3–4 minutes, stirring once or twice.

Add the wine, vinegar and reserved pasta to the pan, stir and bring the mixture just to the boil over a medium heat.

Arrange the salad leaves on large serving plates, spoon over the warm sausage and pasta mixture and serve immediately.

SERVES 6

225 g/8 oz dried fusilli
4 tomatoes, peeled
55 g/2 oz black olives
25 g/1 oz sun-dried
  tomatoes in oil, drained
2 tbsp pine kernels,
  toasted
salt

1 fresh basil sprig,
  to garnish
2 tbsp freshly grated
  Parmesan cheese,
  to serve

pesto vinaigrette
1 garlic clove, very finely
  chopped

4 tbsp chopped fresh
  basil
2 tbsp freshly grated
  Parmesan cheese
4 tbsp olive oil
2 tbsp lemon juice
pepper

Pasta Salad with Pesto Vinaigrette

Bring a large saucepan of lightly salted water to the boil over a medium heat. Add the pasta and cook for about 8–10 minutes, or until tender but still firm to the bite. Drain, rinse in hot water, then drain again and reserve.

To make the pesto vinaigrette, whisk the garlic, basil, Parmesan cheese, oil and lemon juice together in a small bowl until well blended. Season to taste with pepper.

Put the pasta into a bowl, pour over the pesto vinaigrette and toss thoroughly.

Cut the tomatoes into wedges. Halve and stone the olives and slice the sun-dried tomatoes. Add the tomatoes, olives and sun-dried tomatoes to the pasta and toss well.

Transfer the pasta mixture to a salad bowl and garnish with a fresh basil sprig. Scatter the pine kernels and Parmesan cheese over the top and serve warm.

SERVES 4-6

225 g/8 oz pasta shapes, such as farfalle or fusilli

5 spring onions, some green included, sliced

250 g/9 oz shelled baby broad beans (frozen or fresh)

100 g/3½ oz chorizo, thinly sliced

6 tbsp extra virgin olive oil

2 shallots, finely chopped

2 tbsp red wine vinegar

2 tbsp chopped fresh thyme or marjoram

squeeze of lemon juice

¼ tsp dried chilli flakes

salt and pepper

Broad Bean, Chorizo & Pasta Salad

Bring a large saucepan of lightly salted water to the boil over a medium heat. Add the pasta and cook for 8–10 minutes, or until tender but still firm to the bite. Drain and transfer to a serving dish. Add the spring onions, tossing to mix.

Meanwhile, put the broad beans in a pan of boiling water. Bring back to the boil and cook for 4 minutes if frozen, 3 minutes if fresh, or until just tender. Drain under cold running water and pat dry with paper towels. Peel away the outer skins if they are tough. Mix with the pasta and spring onions.

Cut the chorizo slices into quarters. Heat a large frying pan over medium–high heat. Fry the chorizo in a single layer for 3–4 minutes until beginning to blacken slightly. Add to the pasta mixture and toss well.

Reduce the heat to medium–low and warm the olive oil. Add the shallots and gently fry for 2 minutes until soft. Swirl in the vinegar and cook for a few seconds more. Tip the contents of the pan over the pasta mixture and toss to coat.

Stir in the herbs, lemon juice, chilli flakes and season to taste with salt and pepper. Toss thoroughly to mix, then leave to stand at room temperature for 30 minutes to allow the flavour to develop. Toss again and add more seasoning if necessary. Serve at room temperature.

SERVES 4

250 g/9 oz dried penne
1 head radicchio, torn
  into pieces
1 Webbs lettuce, torn into
  pieces
7 tbsp chopped walnuts
2 ripe pears, cored and
  diced

115 g/4 oz rocket
2 tbsp lemon juice
5 tbsp olive oil
1 garlic clove, chopped
3 tbsp white wine vinegar
4 tomatoes, cut into
  wedges

1 small onion, sliced
1 large carrot, grated
250 g/9 oz goat's cheese,
  diced
salt

Penne with Goat's Cheese, Pears & Walnuts

Bring a large saucepan of lightly salted water to the boil over a medium heat. Add the pasta and cook for about 8–10 minutes, or until tender but still firm to the bite. Drain the pasta, refresh under cold running water, drain again and leave to cool.

Put the radicchio and Webbs lettuce into a large salad bowl and mix together well. Top with the cooled pasta, walnuts, pears and rocket.

Mix the lemon juice, oil, garlic and vinegar together in a measuring jug. Pour the mixture over the salad ingredients and toss to coat the salad leaves thoroughly.

Add the tomato wedges, onion slices, grated carrot and diced goat's cheese and, using 2 forks, toss together until well mixed. Leave the salad to chill in the refrigerator for about 1 hour before serving.

SERVES 4

225 g/8 oz dried farfalle
6 pieces of sun-dried
 tomato in oil, drained
 and chopped
4 spring onions, chopped
55 g/2 oz rocket,
 shredded

½ cucumber, deseeded
 and diced
salt and pepper
2 tbsp freshly grated
 Parmesan cheese,
 to serve

dressing
4 tbsp olive oil
1 tbsp white wine vinegar
½ tsp caster sugar
1 tsp Dijon mustard
4 fresh basil leaves, finely
 shredded
salt and pepper

Warm Pasta Salad

To make the dressing, whisk the oil, vinegar, sugar and mustard together in a jug. Season to taste with salt and pepper and stir in the basil.

Bring a large saucepan of lightly salted water to boil over a medium heat. Add the pasta, bring back to the boil and cook for 8–10 minutes, or until tender but still firm to the bite. Drain and transfer to a salad bowl. Add the dressing and toss well.

Add the sun-dried tomatoes, spring onions, rocket and cucumber, season to taste with salt and pepper and toss. Sprinkle with the Parmesan cheese and serve warm.

SERVES 4

250 g/9 oz dried orecchiette
1 head radicchio, torn into pieces
1 looseleaf lettuce, torn into pieces
2 pears
1 tbsp lemon juice

250 g/9 oz Stilton cheese, diced
55 g/2 oz walnuts, chopped
4 tomatoes, quartered
1 red onion, sliced
1 carrot, grated
8 fresh basil leaves

55 g/2 oz lamb's lettuce

dressing
4 tbsp olive oil
2 tbsp lemon juice
1 tbsp white wine vinegar
salt and pepper

Orecchiette Salad with Pears & Stilton

Bring a large saucepan of lightly salted water to boil over a medium heat. Add the pasta, return to the boil and cook for 8–10 minutes, or until tender but still firm to the bite. Drain, refresh in a bowl of cold water and drain again.

Place the radicchio and looseleaf lettuce leaves in a salad bowl. Halve the pears, remove the cores and dice the flesh. Toss the diced pear with 1 tablespoon of lemon juice in a small bowl to prevent discoloration. Top the salad with the Stilton, walnuts, pears, pasta, tomatoes, onion slices and grated carrot. Add the basil and lamb's lettuce.

For the dressing, mix the olive oil and the lemon juice and vinegar together in a jug, then season to taste with salt and pepper. Pour the dressing over the salad, toss and serve.

SERVES 4	2 large lettuces	juice of 4 lemons	250 ml/9 fl oz fresh garlic
	250 g/9 oz dried penne	1 head of celery, sliced	mayonnaise
	8 red apples, diced	115 g/4 oz walnut halves	salt and pepper

Penne & Apple Salad

Wash and drain the lettuce leaves, then pat them dry with kitchen paper. Transfer them to the refrigerator for 1 hour, or until crisp.

Meanwhile, bring a large saucepan of lightly salted water to the boil over a medium heat. Add the pasta, bring back to the boil and cook for 8–10 minutes, or until tender but still firm to the bite. Drain the pasta and refresh under cold running water. Drain thoroughly and cool.

Place the apples in a bowl and sprinkle with the lemon juice to coat them thoroughly – this will prevent discoloration. Mix together the cooled pasta, celery, apples and walnut halves and toss the mixture in the garlic mayonnaise. Season to taste with salt and pepper.

Line a salad bowl with the lettuce leaves and spoon the pasta salad on top. Refrigerate until ready to serve.

SERVES 6

225 g/8 oz dried green fusilli
5 tbsp extra virgin olive oil
450 g/1 lb cooked prawns
1 Charentais melon

1 Galia melon
1 tbsp red wine vinegar
1 tsp Dijon mustard
pinch of caster sugar
1 tbsp chopped fresh flat-leaf parsley

1 tbsp chopped fresh basil, plus extra sprigs to garnish
1 loose-leaf or quattro stagioni lettuce, shredded
salt and pepper

Pasta Salad with Melon + Prawns

Bring a large saucepan of lightly salted water to boil over a medium heat. Add the pasta, bring back to the boil and cook for 8–10 minutes, until tender but still firm to the bite. Drain, toss with 1 tablespoon of the oil and leave to cool.

Meanwhile, peel and devein the prawns, then place them in a large bowl. Halve both the melons and scoop out the seeds with a spoon. Using a melon baller or teaspoon, scoop out balls of the flesh and add them to the prawns.

Whisk together the remaining oil, the vinegar, mustard, sugar, parsley and chopped basil in a small bowl. Season to taste with salt and pepper. Add the cooled pasta to the prawn and melon mixture and toss lightly to mix, then pour in the dressing and toss again. Cover with clingfilm and chill in the refrigerator for 30 minutes.

Make a bed of shredded lettuce on a serving plate. Spoon the pasta salad on top, garnish with basil sprigs and serve.

SERVES 4	115 g/4 oz french beans, cut into 5-cm/2-inch lengths	6 cherry tomatoes, halved	3 tbsp chopped fresh flat-leaf parsley
	225 g/8 oz dried fusilli	55 g/2 oz black olives, stoned and halved	2 tbsp lemon juice
	100 ml/3½ fl oz olive oil	6 canned anchovies, drained and chopped	8–10 radicchio leaves
	2 tuna steaks, about 350 g/12 oz each		salt and pepper

Pasta Niçoise

Bring a large saucepan of lightly salted water to boil over a medium heat. Add the French beans, reduce the heat and cook for 5–6 minutes. Remove with a slotted spoon and refresh in a bowl of cold water. Drain well. Add the pasta to the same pan, return to the boil and cook for 8–10 minutes, or until the pasta is tender but still firm to the bite.

Meanwhile, brush a griddle pan with some of the olive oil and heat until smoking. Season the tuna to taste with salt and pepper and brush both sides with some of the remaining olive oil. Cook over a medium heat for 2 minutes on each side, or until cooked to your liking, then remove from the griddle pan and reserve.

Drain the pasta well and tip it into a bowl. Add the beans, tomatoes, olives, anchovies, parsley, lemon juice and remaining olive oil and season to taste with salt and pepper. Toss well and leave to cool. Remove and discard any skin from the tuna and break into chunks.

Gently mix the tuna into the pasta salad. Line a large salad bowl with the radicchio leaves, spoon in the salad and serve.

SERVES 2

100 g/3½ oz small wholewheat pasta shapes
2 tbsp olive oil, plus extra if needed
1 tbsp mayonnaise
1 tbsp natural yogurt

2 tbsp pesto
200 g/7 oz canned tuna in spring water, drained and flaked
200 g/7 oz canned no-added-sugar sweetcorn kernels, drained

2 tomatoes, peeled, deseeded and chopped
½ green pepper, deseeded and chopped
½ avocado, stoned, peeled and chopped
salt and pepper

Tuna & Pasta Salad

Bring a large saucepan of lightly salted water to the boil over a medium heat. Add the pasta and cook for 8–10 minutes, until just tender. Drain, return to the saucepan and add half the oil. Toss well to coat, then cover and leave to cool.

Whisk the mayonnaise, yogurt and pesto together in a jug, adding a little oil if needed to achieve the desired consistency. Season to taste with salt and pepper.

Mix the pasta with the tuna, sweetcorn, tomatoes, green pepper and avocado, add the dressing and toss well to coat.

SERVES 4		
450 g/1 lb prepared squid, cut into strips	300 ml/10 fl oz olive oil	1 bunch fresh parsley, finely chopped
750 g/1 lb 10 oz cooked mussels	225 g/8 oz dried campanelle or other small pasta shapes	salt and pepper
450 g/1 lb cooked cockles in brine	juice of 1 lemon	mixed salad leaves, to serve
150 ml/5 fl oz white wine	1 bunch chives, snipped	4 large tomatoes, to garnish

Neapolitan Seafood Salad

Put all of the seafood into a large bowl, pour over the wine and half of the olive oil, and set aside for 6 hours.

Put the seafood mixture into a saucepan and simmer over a low heat for 10 minutes. Set aside to cool.

Bring a large saucepan of lightly salted water to the boil over a medium heat. Add the pasta and 1 tbsp of the remaining olive oil and cook for 8–10 minutes, or until tender but still firm to the bite. Drain thoroughly and refresh in cold water.

Strain off about half of the cooking liquid from the seafood and discard the rest. Mix in the lemon juice, chives, parsley and the remaining olive oil. Season to taste with salt and pepper. Drain the pasta and add to the seafood.

Shred the leaves and arrange them at the base of a salad bowl. Cut the tomatoes into quarters. Spoon the seafood salad into the bowl, garnish with the tomatoes and serve.

Meat & Poultry

SERVES 4

1 tbsp olive oil
1 onion, finely chopped
2 garlic cloves, chopped
1 carrot, chopped
1 celery stick, chopped
50 g/1¾ oz pancetta or
  streaky bacon, diced

350 g/12 oz fresh lean
  beef mince
400 g/14 oz canned
  chopped tomatoes
2 tsp dried oregano
125 ml/4 fl oz red wine
2 tbsp tomato purée

350 g/12 oz dried
  spaghetti
salt and pepper
chopped fresh parsley,
  to garnish

Spaghetti Bolognese

Heat the oil in a large frying pan. Add the onion and cook for 3 minutes. Add the garlic, carrot, celery and pancetta and cook for 3–4 minutes, or until just beginning to brown.

Add the beef and cook over a high heat for a further 3 minutes, or until the meat has browned. Stir in the tomatoes, oregano and red wine and bring to the boil. Reduce the heat and leave to simmer for about 45 minutes.

Stir in the tomato purée and season to taste with salt and pepper.

Bring a large saucepan of lightly salted water to boil over a medium heat. Add the pasta and cook for 8–10 minutes, or until tender but still firm to the bite. Drain thoroughly.

Transfer the spaghetti to a serving plate and pour over the bolognese sauce. Toss to mix well, garnish with parsley and serve hot.

SERVES 6

175 ml/6 fl oz olive oil
55 g/2 oz butter
85 g/3 oz pancetta, diced
1 onion, finely chopped
1 celery stick, finely
  chopped
1 carrot, finely chopped
350 g/12 oz beef topside
  in a single piece

5 tbsp red wine
2 tbsp sun-dried tomato
  paste
200 g/7 oz Italian sausage
2 eggs
115 g/4 oz Parmesan
  cheese, freshly grated
25 g/1 oz fresh
  breadcrumbs

350 g/12 oz ricotta
  cheese
8 sheets dried lasagne
350 g/12 oz mozzarella
  cheese, sliced
salt and pepper
chopped fresh parsley,
  to garnish

Beef Lasagne with Ricotta & Mozzarella

Heat 100 ml/3½ fl oz of the oil with the butter in a large saucepan. Add the pancetta, onion, celery and carrot and cook over a low heat until softened. Increase the heat to medium, add the beef and cook until evenly browned. Stir in the wine and sun-dried tomato paste, season to taste with salt and pepper and bring to the boil. Reduce the heat, cover and simmer gently, stirring occasionally, for 1½ hours, until the beef is tender.

Meanwhile, heat 2 tablespoons of the remaining oil in a frying pan. Add the sausage and cook for 8–10 minutes. Remove from the pan, remove and discard the skin, then thinly slice.

Transfer the beef to a chopping board and dice finely. Return half the beef to the sauce. Mix the remaining beef with 1 egg, 1 tablespoon of the Parmesan and the breadcrumbs. Shape the mixture into walnut-sized balls. Heat the remaining oil in a frying pan, add the meatballs and cook for 5–8 minutes, until browned.

Pass the ricotta through a sieve into a bowl. Stir in the remaining egg and 4 tablespoons of the remaining Parmesan.

Preheat the oven to 180°C/350°F/Gas Mark 4. In a rectangular ovenproof dish make layers of lasagne sheets, ricotta mixture, meat sauce, meatballs, sausage and mozzarella. Finish with a layer of the ricotta mixture and sprinkle with the remaining Parmesan. Bake in the preheated oven for 20–25 minutes, until golden brown. Serve, garnished with parsley.

SERVES 6

1 potato, diced
400 g/14 oz fresh beef
    mince
1 onion, finely chopped
1 egg
4 tbsp chopped fresh
    flat-leaf parsley

plain flour, for dusting
5 tbsp olive oil
400 ml/14 fl oz passata
2 tbsp tomato purée
400 g/14 oz dried
    spaghetti

salt and pepper
freshly grated Parmesan
    cheese, to serve
shredded fresh basil,
    to garnish

Spaghetti with Meatballs

Place the potato in a small pan, add cold water to cover and a pinch of salt
and bring to the boil. Cook for 10–15 minutes, until tender, then drain. Either mash
thoroughly with a potato masher or fork, or pass through a potato ricer.

Combine the potato, beef, onion, egg and parsley in a bowl and season to taste
with salt and pepper. Spread out the flour on a plate. With dampened hands, shape
the meat mixture into walnut-sized balls and roll in the flour. Shake off any excess.

Heat the oil in a heavy-based frying pan, add the meatballs and cook over a
medium heat, stirring and turning frequently, for 8–10 minutes, until golden all over.

Add the passata and tomato purée and cook for a further 10 minutes, until the
sauce is reduced and thickened.

Meanwhile, bring a large saucepan of lightly salted water to the boil over a
medium heat. Add the pasta, bring back to the boil and cook for 8–10 minutes, or
until tender but still firm to the bite.

Drain well and add to the meatball sauce, tossing well to coat. Transfer to a warmed
serving dish, top with the Parmesan, garnish with the basil and serve immediately.

SERVES 6

3 tbsp olive oil
70 g/2½ oz butter
350 g/12 oz stewing beef, in a single piece
1 red onion, finely chopped
1 celery stick, finely chopped

1 carrot, finely chopped
150 ml/5 fl oz red wine
225 ml/8 fl oz beef stock
1 tbsp tomato purée
55 g/2 oz fresh breadcrumbs
4 tbsp freshly grated Parmesan cheese

pinch of freshly grated nutmeg
pinch of ground cinnamon
2 eggs, lightly beaten
1½ quantities Basic Pasta Dough (see p6)
plain flour, for dusting
salt and pepper

Beef Ravioli

Heat the oil and half the butter in a large saucepan. Add the beef and cook over a medium heat for 8–10 minutes. Remove the beef from the pan. Reduce the heat and add the onion, celery and carrot to the pan. Cook for 5 minutes, until softened. Return the beef to the pan, add the wine and cook until reduced by two thirds. Combine the stock and tomato purée, stir into the pan and season. Cover and simmer very gently for 3 hours, until the meat is tender and the sauce has thickened. Remove the beef from the pan and leave to cool slightly.

Mix the breadcrumbs and half the Parmesan together and stir in about half the sauce (discard the remaining sauce). Finely chop the beef and stir it into the breadcrumb mixture. Season to taste with salt and pepper and stir in the nutmeg, cinnamon and eggs.

Roll out the pasta dough on a lightly floured surface to 2–3 mm/1⁄16–1⁄8 inch thick. Using a fluted 5-cm/2-inch biscuit cutter, stamp out rounds. Place about 1 teaspoon of the beef mixture in the centre of each round, brush the edges with water, and fold in half, pressing the edges to seal. Place on a floured tea towel and leave to stand for 30 minutes.

Bring a large saucepan of lightly salted water to the boil over a medium heat. Add the ravioli and cook for 5–8 minutes, until tender. Meanwhile, melt the remaining butter. Drain the ravioli and place in a serving dish. Pour over the melted butter, sprinkle with the remaining Parmesan and serve.

SERVES 4	750 g/1 lb 10 oz boneless lean lamb in a single piece	6–8 fresh rosemary sprigs	175 g/6 oz button mushrooms
		125 ml/4 fl oz olive oil	salt and pepper
	6 garlic cloves, thinly sliced	400 g/14 oz dried tagliatelle	fresh pecorino cheese shavings, to serve
		55 g/2 oz butter	

Tagliatelle with Lamb

Using a sharp knife, cut small pockets all over the lamb, then insert a garlic slice and a few rosemary leaves in each one. Heat 2 tablespoons of the oil in a large heavy-based frying pan. Add the lamb and cook over a medium heat, turning occasionally, for 25–30 minutes, until tender and cooked to your liking.

Meanwhile, chop the remaining rosemary and place in a mortar. Add the remaining oil and pound with a pestle. Season to taste with salt and pepper and set aside.

Remove the lamb from the heat, cover with foil and leave to stand. Bring a large saucepan of lightly salted water to boil over a medium heat. Add the pasta, bring back to the boil and cook for 8–10 minutes, until tender but still firm to the bite.

Meanwhile, melt the butter in another pan. Add the mushrooms and cook over a medium–low heat, stirring occasionally, for 5–8 minutes, until tender.

Drain the pasta, return it to the pan and toss with half the rosemary oil. Uncover the lamb and cut it into slices. Divide the tagliatelle between individual warmed plates, season with pepper and top with the lamb and mushrooms. Drizzle with the remaining rosemary oil, sprinkle with the pecorino cheese and serve immediately.

SERVES 4

1 tbsp olive oil
1 onion, chopped
2 garlic cloves, finely chopped
450 g/1 lb fresh lamb mince

2 tbsp tomato purée
2 tbsp plain flour
300 ml/10 fl oz chicken stock
1 tsp ground cinnamon
115 g/4 oz dried macaroni

2 beef tomatoes, sliced
300 ml/10 fl oz Greek yogurt
2 eggs, lightly beaten
salt and pepper

Pasticcio

Preheat the oven to 190°C/375°F/Gas Mark 5. Heat the oil in a large heavy-based frying pan. Add the onion and garlic and cook over a low heat, stirring occasionally, for 5 minutes, or until softened. Add the lamb and cook, breaking it up with a wooden spoon, until browned all over. Add the tomato purée and sprinkle in the flour. Cook, stirring, for 1 minute, then stir in the stock. Season to taste with salt and pepper and stir in the cinnamon. Bring to the boil, reduce the heat, cover and cook for 25 minutes.

Bring a large saucepan of lightly salted water to boil over a medium heat. Add the pasta, return to the boil and cook for 8–10 minutes, or until tender but still firm to the bite.

Drain the pasta and stir into the lamb mixture. Spoon into a large ovenproof dish and arrange the tomato slices on top. Beat together the yogurt and eggs then spoon over the lamb evenly. Bake in the preheated oven for 1 hour and then serve immediately.

SERVES 4

4 tbsp olive oil	400 g/14 oz dried rigatoni	1 tbsp chopped fresh
1 red onion, chopped	280 g/10 oz chorizo	coriander
1 garlic clove, chopped	sausage, sliced	1 tbsp lime juice
1 celery stick, sliced	225 g/8 oz chestnut	salt and pepper
	mushrooms, halved	

Rigatoni with Chorizo & Mushrooms

Heat the oil in a frying pan. Add the onion, garlic and celery and cook over a low heat, stirring occasionally, for 5 minutes, until softened.

Meanwhile, bring a large saucepan of lightly salted water to the boil over a medium heat. Add the pasta, bring back to the boil and cook for 8–10 minutes, or until tender but still firm to the bite.

While the pasta is cooking, add the chorizo to the frying pan and cook, stirring occasionally, for 5 minutes, until evenly browned. Add the mushrooms and cook, stirring occasionally, for a further 5 minutes. Stir in the coriander and lime juice and season to taste with salt and pepper.

Drain the pasta and return it to the pan. Add the chorizo and mushroom mixture and toss lightly. Divide among individual warmed plates and serve immediately.

SERVES 4

3 tbsp olive oil
1 onion, chopped
1 red pepper, deseeded
and diced
1 orange pepper,
deseeded and diced

800 g/1 lb 12 oz canned
chopped tomatoes
1 tbsp sun-dried tomato
paste
1 tsp paprika
225 g/8 oz pepperoni
sausage, sliced

2 tbsp chopped fresh
flat-leaf parsley, plus
extra to garnish
450 g/1 lb dried penne
salt and pepper

Pepperoni Pasta

Heat 2 tablespoons of the oil in a large heavy-based frying pan. Add the onion and cook over a low heat, stirring occasionally, for 5 minutes, or until softened. Add the red and orange peppers, tomatoes and their can juices, sun-dried tomato paste and paprika and bring to the boil.

Add the pepperoni and parsley and season to taste with salt and pepper. Stir well, bring to the boil, then reduce the heat and simmer for 10–15 minutes.

Meanwhile, bring a large saucepan of lightly salted water to the boil over a medium heat. Add the pasta, return to the boil and cook for 8–10 minutes, or until tender but still firm to the bite. Drain well and transfer to a warmed serving dish. Add the remaining olive oil and toss. Add the sauce and toss again. Sprinkle with parsley and serve immediately.

SERVES 4	450 g/1 lb dried spaghetti	225 g/8 oz rindless pancetta or streaky	5 tbsp single cream
	1 tbsp olive oil	bacon, chopped	2 tbsp freshly grated Parmesan cheese
		4 eggs	salt and pepper

Spaghetti Alla Carbonara

Bring a large saucepan of lightly salted water to boil over a medium heat. Add the pasta, return to the boil and cook for 8–10 minutes, or until tender but still firm to the bite.

Meanwhile, heat the oil in a heavy-based frying pan. Add the pancetta and cook over a medium heat, stirring frequently, for 8–10 minutes.

Beat the eggs with the cream in a small bowl and season to taste with salt and pepper. Drain the pasta and return it to the saucepan. Tip in the contents of the frying pan, then add the egg mixture and half the Parmesan cheese. Stir well, then transfer to a warmed serving dish. Serve immediately, sprinkled with the remaining cheese.

SERVES 6

1 tbsp olive oil
4 rashers streaky bacon
   or pancetta
115 g/4 oz mushrooms,
   sliced

225 g/8 oz dried fusilli
2 eggs, beaten
115 g/4 oz Cheddar or
   mozzarella cheese,
   cubed

salt and pepper
chopped fresh flat-leaf
   parsley, to garnish

Fusilli with Bacon, Eggs & Mushrooms

Heat the oil in a frying pan over a medium heat. Add the bacon and fry until crisp. Remove with tongs, cut into small pieces and keep warm.

Fry the mushrooms in the pan with the bacon fat for 5–7 minutes until soft. Remove from the heat.

Bring a large saucepan of lightly salted water to boil over a medium heat. Add the pasta and cook for 8–10 minutes, or until tender but still firm to the bite. Drain and keep warm.

Stir the mushrooms, beaten eggs and the cheese cubes into the pasta. Season with pepper and toss until the eggs have coated the pasta and the cheese has melted.

Transfer to a warm serving dish. Sprinkle with the bacon pieces and parsley and serve immediately.

SERVES 4

225 ml/8 fl oz crème fraîche
225 g/8 oz chestnut mushrooms, quartered
400 g/14 oz dried farfalle

85 g/3 oz Gorgonzola cheese, crumbled
1 tbsp chopped fresh flat-leaf parsley, plus extra sprigs to garnish

175 g/6 oz cooked ham, diced
salt and pepper

Farfalle with Gorgonzola & Ham

Pour the crème fraîche into a saucepan, add the mushrooms and season to taste with salt and pepper. Bring to just below the boil, then lower the heat and simmer very gently, stirring occasionally, for 8–10 minutes, until thickened.

Meanwhile, bring a large saucepan of lightly salted water to boil over a medium heat. Add the pasta, bring back to the boil and cook for 8–10 minutes, until tender but still firm to the bite.

Remove the pan containing the mushroom mixture from the heat and stir in the Gorgonzola cheese until it has melted. Return the pan to a very low heat and stir in the chopped parsley and ham.

Drain the pasta and add it to the sauce. Toss lightly, then divide between individual warmed plates, garnish with parsley sprigs and serve.

SERVES 4

2 tbsp olive oil
2 onions, chopped
2 garlic cloves, finely
  chopped
1 tbsp shredded fresh
  basil

800 g/1 lb 12 oz canned
  chopped tomatoes
1 tbsp tomato purée
10–12 dried cannelloni
  tubes
butter, for greasing
225 g/8 oz ricotta cheese

115 g/4 oz cooked ham,
  diced
1 egg
55 g/2 oz freshly grated
  pecorino cheese
salt and pepper

Cannelloni with Ham + Ricotta

Preheat the oven to 180°C/350°F/Gas Mark 4. Heat the oil in a large heavy-based frying pan. Add the onions and garlic and cook over a low heat, stirring occasionally, for 5 minutes, or until the onion is softened. Add the basil, tomatoes and their can juices and tomato purée and season to taste with salt and pepper. Reduce the heat and simmer for 30 minutes, or until thickened.

Meanwhile, bring a large saucepan of lightly salted water to boil over a medium heat. Add the cannelloni tubes, return to the boil and cook for 8–10 minutes, or until tender but still firm to the bite. Using a slotted spoon, transfer the cannelloni tubes to a large plate and pat dry with kitchen paper.

Grease a large, shallow ovenproof dish with butter. Mix the ricotta, ham and egg together in a bowl and season to taste with salt and pepper. Using a teaspoon, fill the cannelloni tubes with the ricotta mixture and place in a single layer in the dish. Pour the tomato sauce over the cannelloni and sprinkle with the grated pecorino cheese. Bake in the preheated oven for 30 minutes, or until golden brown. Serve immediately.

SERVES 4

1 tbsp olive oil
2 tbsp butter
1 onion, finely chopped
150 g/5½ oz ham, diced
2 garlic cloves, very finely chopped

1 fresh red chilli, deseeded and finely chopped
800 g/1 lb 12 oz canned chopped tomatoes
450 g/1 lb dried penne

2 tbsp chopped fresh flat-leaf parsley
salt and pepper
6 tbsp freshly grated Parmesan cheese, plus extra to serve

Penne with Ham, Tomato & Chilli Sauce

Put the oil and 1 tablespoon of the butter in a large saucepan over a medium–low heat. Add the onion and cook for 10 minutes, or until soft and golden. Add the ham and cook for 5 minutes, or until lightly browned. Stir in the garlic, chilli and tomatoes. Season to taste with salt and pepper. Bring to the boil, then simmer over a medium–low heat for 30–40 minutes, until thickened.

Meanwhile, bring a large saucepan of lightly salted water to boil over a medium heat. Add the pasta, return to the boil and cook for 8–10 minutes, or until tender but still firm to the bite. Drain and transfer to a warmed serving dish.

Pour the sauce over the pasta. Add the parsley, Parmesan cheese and the remaining butter. Toss well to mix and serve immediately, sprinkled with more Parmesan cheese.

SERVES 4

450 g/1 lb pork fillet, thinly sliced
4 tbsp olive oil
225 g/8 oz button mushrooms, sliced
1 tbsp lemon juice
pinch of saffron threads

350 g/12 oz dried orecchiette
4 tbsp double cream
salt
12 quail eggs, to garnish

red wine sauce
1 tbsp olive oil
1 onion, chopped
1 tbsp tomato purée
200 ml/7 fl oz red wine
1 tsp finely chopped fresh oregano

Pasta & Pork in Cream Sauce

To make the red wine sauce, heat the oil in a small heavy-based saucepan, add the onion and cook until translucent. Stir in the tomato purée, red wine and oregano. Heat gently to reduce and set aside.

Pound the slices of pork between 2 sheets of clingfilm until wafer thin, then cut into strips. Heat the oil in a frying pan, add the pork and cook for 5 minutes. Add the mushrooms and cook for a further 2 minutes. Strain and pour over the red wine sauce. Reduce the heat and simmer for 20 minutes.

Meanwhile, bring a large saucepan of lightly salted water to boil over a medium heat. Add the lemon juice, saffron and pasta, return to the boil and cook for 8–10 minutes, or until tender but still firm to the bite. Drain the pasta thoroughly, return to the saucepan and keep warm.

Stir the cream into the saucepan with the pork and heat for a few minutes.

Boil the quail eggs for 3 minutes, cool them in cold water and remove the shells. Transfer the pasta to a large warmed serving plate, top with the pork and the sauce and garnish with the eggs. Serve immediately.

SERVES 4

450 g/1 lb dried tagliatelle
3 tbsp peanut oil
350 g/12 oz pork fillet, cut into thin strips
1 garlic clove, finely chopped
1 bunch of spring onions, sliced
2.5-cm/1-inch piece fresh ginger, grated

2 fresh Thai chillies, deseeded and finely chopped
1 red pepper, deseeded and cut into thin sticks
1 yellow pepper, deseeded and cut into thin sticks
3 courgettes cut into thin sticks

2 tbsp finely chopped peanuts
1 tsp ground cinnamon
1 tbsp oyster sauce
55 g/2 oz creamed coconut, grated
salt and pepper
2 tbsp chopped fresh coriander, to garnish

Chilli Pork with Tagliatelle

Bring a large saucepan of lightly salted water to boil over a medium heat. Add the pasta, return to the boil and cook for 8–10 minutes, or until tender but still firm to the bite.

Meanwhile, heat the peanut oil in a preheated wok or large, heavy-based frying pan. Add the pork and stir-fry for 5 minutes. Add the garlic, spring onions, ginger and Thai chillies and stir-fry for 2 minutes.

Add the red and yellow peppers and the courgettes and stir-fry for 1 minute. Add the peanuts, cinnamon, oyster sauce and creamed coconut and stir-fry for a further 1 minute. Season to taste with salt and pepper. Drain the pasta and transfer to a serving dish. Top with the chilli pork, sprinkle with the chopped coriander and serve.

SERVES 4

2 tbsp olive oil
1 onion, chopped
1 garlic clove, finely
   chopped
2 carrots, diced
55 g/2 oz pancetta,
   chopped
115 g/4 oz mushrooms,
   chopped

450 g/1 lb fresh pork
   mince
125 ml/4 fl oz dry white
   wine
4 tbsp passata
200 g/7 oz canned
   chopped tomatoes
2 tsp chopped fresh
   sage, plus extra sprigs
   to garnish

225 g/8 oz dried penne
140 g/5 oz mozzarella
   cheese, diced
4 tbsp freshly grated
   Parmesan
300 ml/10 fl oz Béchamel
   Sauce
salt and pepper

Pork + Pasta Bake

Preheat the oven to 200°C/400°F/Gas Mark 6. Heat the oil in a large heavy-based frying pan. Add the onion, garlic and carrots and cook over a low heat, stirring occasionally, for 5 minutes, or until the onion has softened. Add the pancetta and cook for 5 minutes. Add the chopped mushrooms and cook, stirring occasionally, for a further 2 minutes. Add the pork and cook, breaking it up with a wooden spoon, until the meat is browned all over. Stir in the wine, passata, chopped tomatoes and their can juices and chopped sage. Season to taste with salt and pepper, bring to the boil, then cover and simmer over a low heat for 25–30 minutes.

Meanwhile, bring a large saucepan of lightly salted water to boil over a medium heat. Add the pasta, return to the boil and cook for 8–10 minutes, or until tender but still firm to the bite.

Spoon the pork mixture into a large ovenproof dish. Stir the mozzarella cheese and half the Parmesan cheese into the Béchamel Sauce. Drain the pasta and stir the sauce into it, then spoon it over the pork mixture. Sprinkle with the remaining Parmesan cheese and bake in the preheated oven for 25–30 minutes, or until golden brown. Serve immediately, garnished with sage sprigs.

SERVES 6

2 tbsp olive oil
900 g/2 lb fresh chicken mince
1 garlic clove, finely chopped
4 carrots, chopped

4 leeks, sliced
450 ml/16 fl oz chicken stock
2 tbsp tomato purée
115 g/4 oz Cheddar cheese, grated

1 tsp Dijon mustard
600 ml/1 pint Béchamel Sauce
8 sheets dried lasagne
salt and pepper

Chicken Lasagne

Preheat the oven to 190°C/375°F/Gas Mark 5. Heat the oil in a heavy-based saucepan. Add the chicken and cook over a medium heat, breaking it up with a wooden spoon, for 5 minutes, or until it is browned all over. Add the garlic, carrots and leeks and cook, stirring occasionally, for 5 minutes.

Stir in the stock and tomato purée and season to taste with salt and pepper. Bring to the boil, reduce the heat, cover and simmer for 30 minutes.

Stir half the Cheddar cheese and the mustard into the hot Béchamel Sauce. In a large ovenproof dish, make alternate layers of the chicken mixture, lasagne sheets and cheese sauce, ending with a layer of cheese sauce. Sprinkle with the remaining Cheddar cheese and bake in the preheated oven for 1 hour, or until golden brown and bubbling. Serve immediately.

SERVES 4

2 tbsp olive oil
450 g/1 lb skinless, boneless chicken breasts, cut into thin strips

6 spring onions, chopped
225 g/8 oz feta cheese, diced
4 tbsp snipped fresh chives

450 g/1 lb dried penne
salt and pepper

Penne with Chicken & Feta Cheese

Heat the oil in a heavy-based frying pan. Add the chicken and cook over a medium heat, stirring frequently, for 5–8 minutes, or until golden all over and cooked through. Add the spring onions and cook for 2 minutes. Stir the feta cheese into the frying pan with half the chives and season to taste with salt and pepper.

Meanwhile, bring a large saucepan of lightly salted water to boil over a medium heat. Add the pasta, return to the boil and cook for 8–10 minutes, or until tender but still firm to the bite. Drain well, then transfer to a warmed serving dish.

Spoon the chicken mixture onto the pasta, toss lightly and serve immediately, garnished with the remaining chives.

SERVES 4

1 tbsp olive oil
thinly pared rind of
   1 lemon, cut into
   julienne strips
1 tsp finely chopped fresh
   ginger
1 tsp sugar

225 ml/8 fl oz chicken
   stock
250 g/9 oz dried
   spaghetti
55 g/2 oz butter
225 g/8 oz skinless,
   boneless chicken
   breasts, diced

1 red onion, finely
   chopped
leaves from 2 bunches of
   flat-leaf parsley
salt

Spaghetti with Parsley Chicken

Heat the oil in a heavy-based saucepan. Add the lemon rind and cook over a low heat, stirring frequently, for 5 minutes. Stir in the ginger and sugar, season to taste with salt and cook, stirring constantly, for a further 2 minutes. Pour in the stock, bring to the boil, then cook for 5 minutes, or until the liquid has reduced by half.

Meanwhile, bring a large saucepan of lightly salted water to boil over a medium heat. Add the pasta, return to the boil and cook for 8–10 minutes, or until tender but still firm to the bite.

Melt half the butter in a frying pan. Add the chicken and onion and cook, stirring frequently, for 5 minutes, or until the chicken is lightly browned all over. Stir in the lemon and ginger mixture and cook for 1 minute. Stir in the parsley leaves and cook, stirring constantly, for a further 3 minutes.

Drain the pasta and transfer to a warmed serving dish, then add the remaining butter and toss well. Add the chicken sauce, toss again and serve.

SERVES 4

115 g/4 oz skinless, boneless chicken breast
55 g/2 oz Parma ham
40 g/1½ oz cooked spinach, well drained
1 tbsp finely chopped onion

6 tbsp freshly grated Parmesan cheese
pinch of ground allspice
2 eggs, beaten
2 quantities Basic Pasta Dough
plain flour, for dusting
300 ml/10 fl oz single cream

2 garlic cloves, crushed
115 g/4 oz button mushrooms, thinly sliced
salt and pepper
2 tbsp chopped fresh parsley, to garnish

Chicken Tortellini

Bring a large saucepan of lightly salted water to boil over a medium heat. Add the chicken and poach for 10 minutes. Leave to cool slightly, then put in a food processor with the Parma ham, spinach and onion and process until finely chopped. Stir in 2 tablespoons of the Parmesan, the allspice and 1 of the eggs and season with salt and pepper.

Roll out the pasta dough on a lightly floured surface to a rectangle 2–3 mm/¹⁄₁₆–⅛ inch thick. Using a 5-cm/2-inch plain biscuit cutter, stamp out rounds. Place about 1 teaspoon of the filling in the centre of each round. Brush the edges with a little beaten egg, then fold in half to make a half moon, pressing the edges to seal. Wrap the half moon around the tip of your index finger until the corners meet and press them together to seal. Repeat with the remaining pasta half moons. Place the filled tortellini on a floured tea towel and leave to stand for 1 hour.

Bring a large saucepan of lightly salted water to boil over a medium heat. Add the tortellini in batches and cook for 10 minutes. Remove with a slotted spoon and drain on kitchen paper, then transfer to a serving dish.

To make the sauce, bring the cream and garlic to the boil in a small pan, then simmer for 3 minutes. Add the mushrooms and 2 tablespoons of the Parmesan cheese, season to taste with salt and pepper and simmer for 2–3 minutes. Pour the sauce over the tortellini. Sprinkle over the remaining Parmesan cheese, garnish with the parsley and serve.

SERVES 4

butter, for greasing
2 tbsp olive oil
2 garlic cloves, crushed
1 large onion, finely
    chopped
225 g/8 oz wild
    mushrooms, sliced

350 g/12 oz fresh chicken
    mince
115 g/4 oz prosciutto,
    diced
150 ml/5 fl oz Marsala
200 g/7 oz canned
    chopped tomatoes
1 tbsp shredded fresh
    basil leaves

2 tbsp tomato purée
10–12 dried cannelloni
    tubes
600 ml/1 pint Béchamel
    Sauce
85 g/3 oz freshly grated
    Parmesan cheese
salt and pepper

Chicken & Mushroom Cannelloni

Preheat the oven to 190°C/375°F/Gas Mark 5. Lightly grease a large ovenproof dish. Heat the oil in a heavy-based frying pan. Add the garlic, onion and mushrooms and cook over a low heat, stirring frequently, for 8–10 minutes. Add the chicken mince and prosciutto and cook, stirring frequently, for 12 minutes, or until browned all over. Stir in the Marsala, tomatoes and their can juices, basil and tomato purée and cook for 4 minutes. Season to taste with salt and pepper, then cover and simmer for 30 minutes. Uncover, stir and simmer for 15 minutes.

Meanwhile, bring a large saucepan of lightly salted water to boil over a medium heat. Add the cannelloni tubes, return to the boil and cook for 8–10 minutes, or until tender but still firm to the bite. Using a slotted spoon, transfer the cannelloni tubes to a plate and pat dry with kitchen paper.

Using a teaspoon, fill the cannelloni tubes with the chicken and mushroom mixture. Transfer them to the greased dish. Pour the Béchamel Sauce over them to cover completely and sprinkle with the grated Parmesan cheese.

Bake in the preheated oven for 30 minutes, or until golden brown and bubbling. Serve immediately.

SERVES 4

450 g/1 lb turkey steaks
grated zest of 1 lemon
2 tsp cracked black
   peppercorns
350 g/12 oz egg
   tagliatelle

1 tbsp olive oil
55 g/2 oz butter
juice of ½ lemon
250 ml/9 fl oz double
   cream

4 tbsp chopped flat leaf
   parsley
salt

Turkey Tagliatelle with Lemon Pepper Cream Sauce

Place the turkey steaks between two sheets of cling film and flatten with a mallet. Slice the meat across the grain into thin strips measuring 1 x 9 cm/½ x 3½ inches. Put the strips in a shallow dish and toss with the lemon zest and the pepper.

Meanwhile, bring a large saucepan of lightly salted water to the boil over a medium heat. Add the pasta, return to the boil and cook for 8-10 minutes, or until tender but still firm to the bite.

Heat the oil and half the butter in a saucepan, and fry the turkey strips for 5 minutes until no longer pink. Season to taste with salt, then transfer to a plate and keep warm.

Add the remaining butter to the pan. Stir in the lemon juice and simmer for a few seconds. Pour in the cream, bring to the boil, then reduce the heat and simmer for 5 minutes, stirring often. Return the turkey to the pan, stirring until well coated with the cream.

Drain the pasta, reserving 4 tablespoons of the cooking water. Tip the pasta into a warmed serving dish. Stir the cooking water into the turkey mixture, then add the parsley. Pour the sauce over the pasta, and toss to mix. Serve immediately.

SERVES 4

115 g/4 oz dried short macaroni
1 small egg, lightly beaten
2 tbsp butter
4 small leeks, green part included, finely sliced
2 carrots, diced

1 tbsp plain flour
¼ tsp freshly grated nutmeg
250 ml/9 fl oz chicken stock
225 g/8 oz diced cooked turkey or chicken
55 g/2 oz diced ham

3 tbsp chopped fresh flat-leaf parsley
100 g/3½ oz freshly grated Gruyère cheese
salt and pepper

Turkey, Leek & Cheese Casserole

Preheat the oven to 180°C/350°F/Gas Mark 4. Bring a large saucepan of lightly salted water to boil over a medium heat. Add the pasta, return to the boil and cook for 8–10 minutes, or until tender but still firm to the bite. Drain and return to the saucepan. Stir in the egg and a knob of the butter, mixing well. Set aside.

Melt the remaining butter in a saucepan over a medium heat. Add the leeks and carrots. Cover and cook for 5 minutes, shaking the saucepan occasionally, until just tender.

Add the flour and nutmeg. Cook for 1 minute, stirring constantly. Pour in the stock. Bring to the boil, stirring constantly. Stir in the turkey, ham and parsley. Season to taste with salt and pepper.

Spread half the turkey mixture over the base of a shallow baking dish. Spread the macaroni over the turkey. Top with the remaining turkey mixture. Sprinkle with the cheese. Bake in the oven for 15–20 minutes. Serve the casserole when the cheese is golden and bubbling.

SERVES 4

350 g/12 oz fresh turkey mince
1 small garlic clove, finely chopped
2 tbsp finely chopped fresh parsley
1 egg, lightly beaten

plain flour, for dusting
3 tbsp olive oil
1 onion, finely chopped
1 celery stick, finely chopped
1 carrot, finely chopped
400 ml/14 fl oz passata

1 fresh rosemary sprig
1 bay leaf
350 g/12 oz dried penne
salt and pepper
freshly grated Parmesan cheese, to serve

Penne with Turkey Meatballs

Put the turkey, garlic and parsley in a bowl and mix well. Stir in the egg and season to taste with salt and pepper. Dust your hands lightly with flour and shape the mixture into walnut-sized balls between your palms. Lightly dust each meatball with flour.

Heat the oil in a saucepan. Add the onion, celery and carrot and cook over a low heat, stirring occasionally, for 5 minutes, until softened. Increase the heat to medium, add the meatballs and cook, turning frequently, for 8–10 minutes, until golden brown all over.

Pour in the passata, add the rosemary and bay leaf, season to taste with salt and pepper and bring to the boil. Lower the heat, cover and simmer gently, stirring occasionally, for 40–45 minutes. Remove and discard the herbs.

Shortly before the meatballs are ready, bring a large saucepan of lightly salted water to boil over a medium heat. Add the pasta, bring back to the boil and cook for 8–10 minutes, until tender but still firm to the bite. Drain and add to the pan with the meatballs. Stir gently and heat through briefly, then spoon into individual warmed dishes. Sprinkle generously with Parmesan cheese and serve immediately.

SERVES 3-4

4 duck legs, halved
125 ml/4 fl oz good-quality balsamic vinegar
2 tbsp olive oil, for frying
1 onion, finely chopped
1 carrot, finely chopped
1 celery stick, finely chopped
1 large garlic clove, finely chopped
125 g/4½ oz chestnut mushrooms, thinly sliced
400 ml/14 fl oz chicken stock
1 tbsp tomato purée
½ tsp dried oregano
squeeze of lemon juice
4 tbsp chopped flat leaf parsley
350 g/12 oz conchiglie
salt and pepper

Conchiglie with Balsamic-Glazed Duck + Mushrooms

Remove the skin from the duck legs and discard. Place the joints in a frying pan and pour in the balsamic vinegar, simmer and turn frequently for 10 minutes. Reduce the heat for 5 minutes then remove the pan from the heat and set aside. Heat the oil in a saucepan and add the onion, carrot, celery and garlic and gently fry over a medium heat until soft but not coloured. Stir in the mushrooms, season with salt and pepper and cook for another 5 minutes then place the duck joints on top of the vegetables.

Pour the stock over the duck then stir in the tomato purée and oregano. Cover and bring to the boil, then reduce the heat and simmer gently for 45–60 minutes, stirring occasionally, until the duck is tender.

Remove the duck from the pan, using tongs. Simmer the sauce for a few minutes until slightly thickened and reduced. Strip the duck meat from the bones, chop it into small pieces and put back in the pan. Add a squeeze of lemon juice, the parsley and season to taste with salt and pepper. Simmer gently for 5 minutes to heat through.

Bring a large saucepan of lightly salted water to boil over a medium heat. Add the pasta, return to the boil and cook for 8–10 minutes, or until tender but still firm to the bite. Drain and transfer to a warmed serving dish. Toss with the sauce and serve immediately.

SERVES 4

4 tbsp olive oil
4 duck legs
1 shallot, finely chopped
1 leek, white part only,
  finely chopped
1 garlic clove, finely
  chopped
1 celery stick, finely
  chopped

1 carrot, finely chopped
4 pancetta or bacon
  slices, diced
1 tbsp finely chopped
  fresh flat-leaf parsley
1 bay leaf
5 tbsp dry white wine
400 g/14 oz canned
  chopped tomatoes

2 tbsp tomato purée
pinch of sugar
450 g/1 lb dried
  fettuccine
salt and pepper
freshly grated Parmesan
  cheese, to serve

Fettuccine with Duck Sauce

Heat half the oil in a frying pan. Add the duck and cook over a medium heat, turning frequently, for 8–10 minutes, until golden brown. Using a slotted spoon, transfer to a large saucepan.

Wipe out the frying pan with kitchen paper, then add the remaining oil. Add the shallot, leek, garlic, celery, carrot and pancetta and cook over a low heat, stirring, for 10 minutes. Using a slotted spoon, transfer the mixture to the pan with the duck and stir in the parsley. Add the bay leaf and season to taste with salt and pepper. Pour in the wine and cook over a high heat, stirring occasionally, until reduced by half. Add the tomatoes, tomato purée and sugar and cook for a further 5 minutes. Pour in just enough water to cover and bring to the boil. Lower the heat, cover and simmer gently for 1 hour, until the duck is cooked through and tender.

Remove the saucepan from the heat and transfer the duck to a chopping board. Skim off the fat from the surface of the sauce and discard the bay leaf. Remove and discard the skin from the duck and cut the meat off the bones, then dice. Return the duck meat to the pan and keep warm.

Bring a large saucepan of lightly salted water to boil over a medium heat. Add the pasta, return to the boil and cook for 8–10 minutes, until tender but still firm to the bite. Drain and place in a serving dish. Adjust the seasoning of the sauce, if necessary, then spoon it on top of the pasta. Sprinkle generously with Parmesan cheese and serve.

Fish & Seafood

SERVES 4

350 g/12 oz dried linguine
2 tbsp olive oil

1 garlic clove, finely chopped
115 g/4 oz smoked salmon, cut into thin strips

55 g/2 oz rocket
salt and pepper
½ lemon, to garnish

Linguine with Smoked Salmon & Rocket

Bring a large saucepan of lightly salted water to boil over a medium heat. Add the pasta, return to the boil and cook for 8–10 minutes, or until tender but still firm to the bite.

Just before the end of the cooking time, heat the olive oil in a heavy-based frying pan. Add the garlic and cook over a low heat for 1 minute, stirring constantly. Do not allow the garlic to brown or it will taste bitter. Add the salmon and rocket. Season to taste with salt and pepper and cook for 1 minute, stirring constantly. Remove the frying pan from the heat.

Drain the pasta and transfer to a warmed serving dish. Add the smoked salmon and rocket mixture, toss lightly and serve, garnished with the lemon half.

SERVES 4

400 g/14 oz dried
  conchiglie
225 g/8 oz broccoli florets
1 tbsp olive oil

2 tbsp butter
1 leek, finely chopped
200 g/7 oz tub garlic and
  herb cream cheese
6 tbsp whole milk

100 g/3½ oz smoked
  salmon pieces
salt and pepper

Creamy Smoked Salmon & Broccoli Pasta

Bring a large saucepan of lightly salted water to the boil over a medium heat. Add the pasta and cook for 8–10 minutes, or until tender but still firm to the bite. Drain and set aside. Meanwhile, steam the broccoli for 8–10 minutes, or until tender.

At the same time, prepare the sauce. Heat the oil and butter in a small heavy-based frying pan, then add the leek and sauté for 7 minutes, or until soft. Gently stir in the cream cheese and milk and heat through.

Add the smoked salmon pieces and cook for a minute or so, until they turn opaque. Combine the sauce with the pasta and broccoli and mix together well. Season to taste with salt and pepper and serve immediately.

SERVES 4

450 g/1 lb dried conchiglie
300 ml/10 fl oz soured cream
2 tsp Dijon mustard

4 large spring onions, finely sliced
225 g/8 oz smoked salmon, cut into bite-sized pieces

finely grated rind of ½ lemon
salt and pepper
2 tbsp snipped fresh chives, to garnish

Conchiglie with Smoked Salmon & Soured Cream

Bring a large saucepan of lightly salted water to the boil over a medium heat. Add the pasta, bring back to the boil and cook for 8–10 minutes, or until tender but still firm to the bite. Drain and return to the pan.

Add the soured cream, mustard, spring onions, smoked salmon and lemon rind to the pasta. Stir over a low heat until heated through. Season to taste with pepper.

Transfer to a serving dish. Sprinkle with the chives and serve.

SERVES 6

350 g/12 oz dried spaghetti
70 g/2½ oz butter, plus extra for greasing
200 g/7 oz smoked salmon, cut into strips

280 g/10 oz large cooked prawns, peeled and deveined
300 ml/10 fl oz Béchamel Sauce

115 g/4 oz freshly grated Parmesan cheese
salt
rocket, to garnish

Layered Salmon & Prawn Spaghetti

Preheat the oven to 180°C/350°F/Gas Mark 4. Butter a large ovenproof dish and set aside.

Bring a large saucepan of lightly salted water to the boil over a medium heat. Add the pasta, bring back to the boil and cook for 8–10 minutes, until tender but still firm to the bite. Drain well, return to the saucepan, add 55 g/2 oz of the butter and toss well.

Spoon half the spaghetti into the prepared dish, cover with the strips of smoked salmon, then top with the prawns. Pour over half the Béchamel Sauce and sprinkle with half the Parmesan cheese. Add the remaining spaghetti, cover with the remaining sauce and sprinkle with the remaining Parmesan cheese. Dice the remaining butter and dot it over the surface.

Bake in the preheated oven for 15 minutes, until the top is golden. Serve immediately, garnished with rocket.

SERVES 4

8 sheets dried lasagne verde
25 g/1 oz butter
1 onion, sliced
½ red pepper, deseeded and chopped
1 courgette, diced
1 tsp chopped fresh ginger

125 g/4½ oz oyster mushrooms, torn into pieces
225 g/8 oz salmon fillet, skinned and cut into chunks
3 tbsp dry sherry
2 tsp cornflour
vegetable oil, for brushing

3 tbsp plain flour
425 ml/15 fl oz milk
25 g/1 oz finely grated Cheddar cheese
1 tbsp fresh white breadcrumbs
salt and pepper
salad leaves, to serve

Salmon Lasagne Rolls

Preheat the oven to 200°C/400°F/Gas Mark 6. Cook the lasagne in a large pan of boiling water for 6 minutes, or according to the instructions on the packet. Remove with tongs and drain on a clean tea towel.

Melt half the butter in a saucepan. Add the onion and cook over a low heat, stirring occasionally, for 5 minutes, until softened. Add the red pepper, courgette and ginger and cook, stirring occasionally, for 10 minutes. Add the mushrooms and salmon and cook for 2 minutes, then mix together the sherry and cornflour and stir into the pan. Cook for a further 4 minutes, until the fish is opaque and flakes easily. Season to taste with salt and pepper and remove the pan from the heat.

Brush an ovenproof dish with oil and set aside. Melt the remaining butter in another pan. Stir in the flour and cook, stirring constantly, for 2 minutes. Gradually stir in the milk, then cook, stirring constantly, for 10 minutes. Remove the pan from the heat, stir in half the Cheddar cheese and season to taste with salt and pepper.

Spoon the salmon filling along one of the shorter sides of each sheet of lasagne. Roll up and place in the prepared dish. Pour the sauce over the rolls and sprinkle with the breadcrumbs and remaining cheese. Bake for 15–20 minutes, until the topping is golden and bubbling. Serve immediately with salad leaves.

SERVES 4-6

85 g/3 oz dried penne or macaroni
2 tsp olive oil, plus extra for coating pasta
1 egg
1 small onion, finely chopped
1 small celery stick, finely chopped
1 small carrot, peeled and finely chopped

small handful of spinach leaves, tough stalks removed and finely shredded
125 ml/4 fl oz milk
2 tbsp double cream
25 g/1 oz mature Cheddar cheese, grated
½ tsp English mustard

1 tbsp finely chopped fresh parsley
squeeze of fresh lemon juice
90 g/3¼ oz undyed smoked haddock, skinned and boned
140 g/5 oz white fish, skinned and boned
85 g/3 oz mozzarella cheese, diced

Two-Fish Casserole

Preheat the oven to 200°C/400°F/Gas Mark 6. Bring a saucepan of lightly salted water to the boil over a medium heat. Add the pasta and cook for 8–10 minutes, or until tender but still firm to the bite. Drain well and toss in oil.

Bring a small saucepan of water to the boil and add the egg. Cook for 8–10 minutes, until the egg is hard boiled. Cool the egg under cold running water.

Heat the oil in a heavy-based frying pan. Add the onion and sauté for 5 minutes, until softened, then add the celery and carrot and sauté for 3 minutes. Add the spinach and cook for a further 2 minutes, until tender.

Stir in the milk and cream and bring to the boil. Turn off the heat and stir in the Cheddar cheese, mustard, parsley and lemon juice.

Place the fish in a small ovenproof dish. Shell and chop the hard-boiled egg and spoon it over the fish, then top with the sauce. Arrange the pasta over the top and sprinkle with the mozzarella cheese. Bake for 20–25 minutes, until brown on top.

SERVES 6

2 carrots, cut into thin batons
2 celery sticks, cut into thin batons
1 courgette, cut into thin batons
1 leek, cut into thin batons

115 g/4 oz fresh or frozen peas
150 ml/5 fl oz vegetable stock
225 g/8 oz smoked trout fillets, skinned and cut into thin strips
200 g/7 oz cream cheese

150 ml/5 fl oz dry white wine
2 tbsp chopped fresh dill, plus extra sprigs to garnish
225 g/8 oz dried tagliatelle
salt and pepper

Creamy Smoked Trout Tagliatelle

Put the carrots, celery, courgette, leek and peas in a large, heavy-based saucepan and pour in the stock. Bring to the boil, then reduce the heat and simmer for 5 minutes, or until the vegetables are tender and most of the stock has evaporated. Remove the pan from the heat, stir in the smoked trout and cover to keep warm.

Put the cheese and wine in a separate large, heavy-based saucepan over a low heat and stir until the cheese has melted and the mixture is smooth. Stir in the chopped dill and season to taste with salt and pepper.

Meanwhile, bring another large saucepan of lightly salted water to boil over a medium heat. Add the pasta, return to the boil and cook for 8–10 minutes, until tender but still firm to the bite. Drain the pasta and tip into the cheese sauce. Toss the pasta using 2 large forks, then transfer to a warmed serving dish. Top with the smoked trout mixture, garnish with the dill sprigs and serve immediately.

SERVES 6

1 tbsp plain flour
450 g/1 lb lemon sole fillets, skinned and cut into chunks
450 g/1 lb monkfish fillets, skinned and cut into chunks
85 g/3 oz unsalted butter

4 shallots, finely chopped
2 garlic cloves, crushed
1 carrot, diced
1 leek, finely chopped
300 ml/10 fl oz fish stock
300 ml/10 fl oz dry white wine

2 tsp anchovy essence
1 tbsp balsamic vinegar
450 g/1 lb dried fettuccine
salt and pepper
chopped fresh flat-leaf parsley, to garnish

Fettuccine with Sole & Monkfish

Spread the flour out on a plate and season with salt and pepper. Coat all the fish pieces with it, shaking off the excess. Melt the butter in a heavy-based saucepan or flameproof casserole. Add the fish, shallots, garlic, carrot and leek, then cook over a low heat, stirring frequently, for 10 minutes. Sprinkle in any remaining seasoned flour and cook, stirring constantly, for 1 minute.

Mix the stock, wine, anchovy essence and vinegar together in a jug and gradually stir into the fish mixture. Bring to the boil, stirring constantly, then reduce the heat and simmer gently for 15 minutes.

Meanwhile, bring a large saucepan of lightly salted water to boil over a medium heat. Add the pasta, return to the boil and cook for 8–10 minutes, or until tender but still firm to the bite. Drain and transfer to a warmed serving dish. Spoon the fish mixture onto the pasta, garnish with chopped parsley and serve immediately.

SERVES 4

115 g/4 oz broccoli, divided into florets
3 tbsp olive oil
350 g/12 oz monkfish fillet, skinned and cut into bite-sized pieces

2 garlic cloves, crushed
125 ml/4 fl oz dry white wine
225 ml/8 fl oz double cream

400 g/14 oz dried fusilli
85 g/3 oz Gorgonzola cheese, diced
salt and pepper

Fusilli with Monkfish & Broccoli

Divide the broccoli florets into tiny sprigs. Bring a saucepan of lightly salted water to the boil, add the broccoli and cook for 2 minutes. Drain and refresh under cold running water.

Heat the oil in a large heavy-based frying pan. Add the monkfish and garlic and season to taste with salt and pepper. Cook, stirring frequently, for 5 minutes, or until the fish is opaque. Pour in the white wine and cream and cook, stirring occasionally, for 5 minutes, or until the fish is cooked through and the sauce has thickened. Stir in the broccoli florets.

Meanwhile, bring a large saucepan of lightly salted water to boil over a medium heat. Add the pasta, return to the boil and cook for 8–10 minutes, or until tender but still firm to the bite. Drain the pasta and tip into the saucepan with the fish, add the Gorgonzola cheese and toss lightly. Serve immediately.

SERVES 3

3 halibut steaks, weighing about 200 g/7 oz each, boned and skinned
200 g/7 oz egg fettuccine
6 tbsp olive oil
25 g/1 oz butter

½ onion, thinly sliced
1 large garlic clove, finely chopped
1½ tbsp capers, drained and rinsed
1 chargrilled red pepper, cut into squares

salt and pepper
1 tbsp chopped flat-leaf parsley, to garnish

Fettuccine with Halibut + Roasted Peppers

Cut the halibut into 2-cm/¾-inch cubes. Pat dry with paper towels and put in a shallow dish. Sprinkle with 1 teaspoon of salt, turning to coat, and set aside.

Bring a large saucepan of lightly salted water to the boil over a medium heat. Add the pasta and cook for 8–10 minutes, or until tender but still firm to the bite. Drain and set aside.

Meanwhile, heat a large frying pan over medium–high heat. Add the oil and butter, and fry the halibut for 2 minutes, turning carefully, until opaque. Season to taste with pepper, then remove to a plate and set aside.

Reduce the heat to medium–low, and gently fry the onion until soft and beginning to colour at the edges. Add the garlic and cook for another 30 seconds, then stir in the capers and pepper. Season to taste with salt and pepper. Return the halibut to the pan and heat through.

Drain the pasta and tip into a warmed serving dish. Spoon the halibut mixture over the top and sprinkle with the parsley. Serve immediately.

SERVES 4

900 g/2 lb fresh, young spinach leaves
400 g/14 oz dried fettuccine

5 tbsp olive oil
3 tbsp pine kernels
3 garlic cloves, crushed

8 canned anchovy fillets, drained and chopped
salt

Spinach & Anchovy Pasta

Trim off any tough spinach stalks. Rinse the spinach leaves under cold running water and place them in a large saucepan with only the water that is clinging to them after washing. Cover and cook over a high heat, shaking the saucepan from time to time, until the spinach has wilted, but retains its colour. Drain well, reserve and keep warm.

Bring a large saucepan of lightly salted water to boil over a medium heat. Add the pasta, return to the boil and cook for 8–10 minutes, or until tender but still firm to the bite.

Meanwhile, heat 4 tablespoons of the oil in a separate saucepan. Add the pine kernels and cook until golden. Remove the pine kernels from the saucepan and reserve until required.

Add the garlic to the saucepan and cook until golden. Add the anchovies and stir in the spinach. Cook, stirring, for 2–3 minutes, until heated through. Return the pine kernels to the saucepan.

Drain the pasta, toss in the remaining oil and transfer to a warmed serving dish. Spoon the anchovy and spinach sauce over the pasta, toss lightly and serve immediately.

SERVES 4

3 tbsp olive oil
2 garlic cloves, finely chopped
10 canned anchovy fillets, drained and chopped

140 g/5 oz black olives, stoned and chopped
1 tbsp capers, drained and rinsed
450 g/1 lb plum tomatoes, peeled, deseeded and chopped

pinch of cayenne pepper
400 g/14 oz dried spaghetti
salt
2 tbsp chopped fresh parsley, to garnish

Spaghetti Alla Puttanesca

Heat the oil in a heavy-based frying pan. Add the garlic and cook over a low heat, stirring frequently, for 2 minutes. Add the anchovies and mash them to a pulp with a fork. Add the olives, capers and tomatoes and season to taste with cayenne pepper. Cover and simmer for 25 minutes.

Meanwhile, bring a large saucepan of lightly salted water to boil over a medium heat. Add the pasta, return to the boil and cook for 8–10 minutes, or until tender but still firm to the bite. Drain well and transfer to a warmed serving dish.

Spoon the anchovy sauce into the dish and toss the pasta, using 2 large forks. Garnish with the chopped parsley and serve immediately.

SERVES 2

140 g/5 oz dried macaroni
1 tbsp olive oil
1 garlic clove, crushed
55 g/2 oz button mushrooms, sliced
½ red pepper, deseeded and thinly sliced

200 g/7 oz canned tuna in brine, drained and flaked
½ tsp dried oregano
25 g/1 oz butter or margarine, plus extra for greasing
1 tbsp plain flour

250 ml/9 fl oz milk
2 tomatoes, sliced
2 tbsp dried breadcrumbs
25 g/1 oz mature Cheddar or Parmesan cheese, grated
salt and pepper

Macaroni & Tuna Bake

Preheat the oven to 200°C/400°F/Gas Mark 6. Bring a large saucepan of lightly salted water to the boil over a medium heat. Add the macaroni, return to the boil and cook for 8–10 minutes, or until tender but still firm to the bite. Drain, rinse and drain again thoroughly.

Heat the oil in a frying pan and cook the garlic, mushrooms and red pepper until soft. Add the tuna and oregano, and season to taste with salt and pepper. Heat through.

Grease a 1-litre/1¾-pint ovenproof dish with a little butter. Add half of the cooked macaroni, cover with the tuna mixture, then add the remaining macaroni.

Melt the butter in a saucepan, stir in the flour and cook for 1 minute. Add the milk gradually and bring to the boil. Simmer for 1–2 minutes, stirring constantly, until thickened. Season to taste with salt and pepper. Pour the sauce over the macaroni. Lay the sliced tomatoes over the sauce and sprinkle with the breadcrumbs and cheese. Cook in the preheated oven for 25 minutes, or until piping hot and the top is well browned.

SERVES 4

200 g/7 oz dried
tagliatelle
25 g/1 oz butter
55 g/2 oz fine fresh
breadcrumbs
400 ml/14 fl oz
condensed canned
cream of mushroom
soup

125 ml/4 fl oz milk
2 celery sticks, chopped
1 red and 1 green
pepper, deseeded and
chopped
140 g/5 oz mature
Cheddar cheese,
roughly grated

2 tbsp chopped fresh
parsley, plus extra sprigs
to garnish
200 g/7 oz canned tuna
in oil, drained and
flaked
salt and pepper

Tuna-Noodle Casserole

Preheat the oven to 200°C/400°F/Gas Mark 6. Bring a large saucepan of lightly salted water to the boil over a medium heat. Add the pasta and cook for 2 minutes less than specified on the packet instructions.

Meanwhile, melt the butter in a small saucepan over a medium heat. Stir in the breadcrumbs, then remove from the heat and reserve.

Drain the pasta well and reserve. Pour the soup into the pasta pan over a medium heat, then stir in the milk, celery, peppers, half the cheese and all the parsley. Add the tuna and gently stir in so that the flakes don't break up. Season to taste with salt and pepper. Heat just until small bubbles appear around the edge of the mixture – do not boil.

Stir the pasta into the pan and use 2 forks to mix all the ingredients together. Spoon the mixture into an ovenproof dish that is also suitable for serving and spread out.

Stir the remaining cheese into the buttered breadcrumbs, then sprinkle over the top of the pasta mixture. Bake in the oven for 20–25 minutes until the topping is golden. Leave to stand for 5 minutes before serving straight from the dish, garnished with the parsley sprigs.

SERVES 4

butter, for greasing
450 g/1 lb dried rigatoni
200 g/7 oz canned
flaked tuna, drained

225 g/8 oz ricotta cheese
125 ml/4 fl oz double
cream
225 g/8 oz freshly grated
Parmesan cheese

115 g/4 oz sun-dried
tomatoes, drained and
sliced
salt and pepper

Baked Tuna & Ricotta Rigatoni

Preheat the oven to 200°C/400°F/Gas Mark 6. Lightly grease a large ovenproof dish with butter. Bring a large saucepan of lightly salted water to boil over a medium heat. Add the rigatoni, return to the boil and cook for 8–10 minutes, or until tender but still firm to the bite. Drain the pasta and leave until cool enough to handle.

Meanwhile, mix the tuna and ricotta cheese together in a bowl to form a soft paste. Spoon the mixture into a piping bag and use to fill the rigatoni. Arrange the filled pasta tubes side by side in the prepared dish.

To make the sauce, mix the cream and Parmesan cheese together in a bowl and season to taste with salt and pepper. Spoon the sauce over the rigatoni and top with the sun-dried tomatoes, arranged in a criss-cross pattern. Bake in the preheated oven for 20 minutes and then serve immediately.

SERVES 4

500 g/1 lb 2 oz dried spaghetti
25 g/1 oz butter
200 g/7 oz canned tuna, drained

55 g/2 oz canned anchovies, drained
250 ml/9 fl oz olive oil
1 large bunch of fresh flat-leaf parsley, roughly chopped

150 ml/5 fl oz crème fraîche
salt and pepper

Spaghetti with Tuna & Parsley

Bring a large saucepan of lightly salted water to boil over a medium heat. Add the spaghetti, return to the boil and cook for 8–10 minutes, or until tender but still firm to the bite. Drain the spaghetti in a colander and return to the saucepan. Add the butter, toss thoroughly to coat and keep warm until required.

Flake the tuna into smaller pieces using 2 forks. Place the tuna in a food processor or blender with the anchovies, oil and parsley and process until the sauce is smooth. Pour in the crème fraîche and process for a few seconds to blend. Taste the sauce and adjust the seasoning, if necessary.

Shake the saucepan of spaghetti over a medium heat for a few minutes, or until it is thoroughly warmed.

Pour the sauce over the spaghetti and toss quickly, using 2 forks. Serve immediately.

SERVES 6

15 g/½ oz butter
225 g/8 oz raw prawns,
  peeled and deveined
450 g/1 lb monkfish fillets,
  skinned and chopped
225 g/8 oz chestnut
  mushrooms, chopped

850 ml/1½ pints
  Béchamel Sauce
400 g/14 oz canned
  chopped tomatoes
1 tbsp chopped fresh
  chervil

1 tbsp shredded fresh
  basil
12 sheets dried lasagne
85 g/3 oz freshly grated
  Parmesan cheese
salt and pepper

Lasagne Alla Marinara

Preheat the oven to 190°C/375°F/Gas Mark 5. Melt the butter in a large
heavy-based saucepan. Add the prawns and monkfish and cook over a medium
heat for 3–5 minutes, or until the prawns change colour. Transfer the prawns to a
small heatproof bowl with a slotted spoon. Add the mushrooms to the saucepan
and cook, stirring occasionally, for 5 minutes. Transfer the fish and mushrooms to the
bowl.

Stir the fish mixture, with any juices, into the Béchamel Sauce and season to taste
with salt and pepper. Layer the tomatoes, chervil, basil, Béchamel Sauce mixture
and lasagne sheets in a large ovenproof dish, ending with a layer of the fish mixture.
Sprinkle evenly with the grated Parmesan cheese.

Bake in the preheated oven for 35 minutes, or until golden brown, then serve
immediately.

SERVES 4

1.5 kg/3 lb 5 oz freshly
  cooked crabmeat,
  shells reserved
2 tbsp virgin olive oil
2 fresh red chillies,
  deseeded and finely
  chopped
4 garlic cloves, finely
  chopped

800 g/1 lb 12 oz canned
  tomatoes
225 ml/8 fl oz dry white
  wine
350 g/12 oz dried
  spaghetti
2 tbsp butter
115 g/4 oz prepared
  squid, sliced

175 g/6 oz raw
  Mediterranean prawns
450 g/1 lb live mussels,
  cleaned
3 tbsp roughly chopped
  fresh flat-leaf parsley
1 tbsp shredded fresh
  basil leaves, plus extra
  sprigs to garnish
salt and pepper

Seafood Pasta Parcels

Carefully break up the larger pieces of crab shell with a meat mallet or the end of a rolling pin. Heat 1 tablespoon of the olive oil in a large saucepan. Add half the chillies and half the garlic, then add the pieces of crab shell. Cook over a medium heat, stirring occasionally, for 2–3 minutes. Add the tomatoes with their can juices and the wine. Reduce the heat and simmer for about 1 hour. Strain the sauce, pressing down on the contents of the sieve with a wooden spoon. Season to taste with salt and pepper and set aside.

Bring a large saucepan of lightly salted water to the boil over a medium heat. Add the pasta, bring back to the boil and cook for 8–10 minutes, until tender but still firm to the bite. Drain and set aside. Heat the remaining oil with the butter in a large, heavy-based saucepan. Add the remaining chilli and garlic and cook over a low heat, stirring occasionally, for 5 minutes, until soft. Add the squid, prawns and mussels, cover and cook over a high heat for 4–5 minutes, until the mussels have opened. Add the crabmeat and heat through for 2–3 minutes. Remove the saucepan from the heat and discard any mussels that remain closed. Add the pasta to the seafood with the chilli and tomato sauce, parsley and basil, tossing well to coat.

Cut out 4 large squares of baking paper or greaseproof paper. Divide the pasta and seafood between them, placing it on one half. Fold over the other half and turn in the edges securely to seal. Transfer to a large baking tray and bake in a preheated oven, 180°C/350°F/Gas Mark 4, for about 10 minutes, until the parcels have puffed up. Serve immediately, garnished with the basil sprigs.

SERVES 4

350 g/12 oz dried macaroni

85 g/3 oz butter, plus extra for greasing

2 small fennel bulbs, trimmed and thinly sliced

175 g/6 oz mushrooms, thinly sliced

175 g/6 oz cooked peeled prawns

pinch of cayenne pepper

600 ml/1 pint Béchamel Sauce

55 g/2 oz freshly grated Parmesan cheese

2 large tomatoes, halved and sliced

olive oil, for brushing

1 tsp dried oregano

salt

Macaroni & Seafood Bake

Preheat the oven to 180°C/350°F/Gas Mark 4. Bring a large saucepan of lightly salted water to boil over a medium heat. Add the pasta, return to the boil and cook for 8–10 minutes, or until tender but still firm to the bite. Drain and return to the saucepan. Add 25 g/1 oz of the butter to the pasta, cover, shake the saucepan and keep warm.

Melt the remaining butter in a separate saucepan. Add the fennel and cook for 3–4 minutes. Stir in the mushrooms and cook for a further 2 minutes. Stir in the prawns, then remove the saucepan from the heat.

Stir the cooked pasta, cayenne pepper and prawn mixture into the Béchamel Sauce.

Grease a large ovenproof dish, then pour the mixture into the dish and spread evenly. Sprinkle over the Parmesan cheese and arrange the tomato slices in a ring around the edge. Brush the tomatoes with oil, then sprinkle over the oregano. Bake in the preheated oven for 25 minutes, or until golden brown. Serve immediately.

SERVES 4

225 g/8 oz dried penne
350 g/12 oz prepared
  squid
6 tbsp olive oil
2 onions, sliced
225 ml/8 fl oz fish stock or
  chicken stock

150 ml/5 fl oz full-bodied
  red wine
400 g/14 oz canned
  chopped tomatoes
2 tbsp tomato purée
1 tbsp chopped fresh
  marjoram

1 bay leaf
salt and pepper
2 tbsp chopped fresh
  parsley, to garnish

Penne with Squid & Tomatoes

Bring a large saucepan of lightly salted water to boil over a medium heat. Add the pasta, return to the boil and cook for 3 minutes, then drain and reserve until required. With a sharp knife, cut the squid into strips.

Heat the olive oil in a large saucepan. Add the onions and cook over a low heat, stirring occasionally, for 5 minutes, or until softened. Add the squid and stock, bring to the boil and simmer for 3 minutes. Stir in the wine, chopped tomatoes and their can juices, tomato purée, marjoram and bay leaf. Season to taste with salt and pepper. Bring to the boil and cook for 5 minutes, or until slightly reduced.

Add the pasta, return to the boil and simmer for 8–10 minutes, or until tender but still firm to the bite. Remove and discard the bay leaf. Transfer to a warmed serving dish, garnish with the parsley and serve immediately.

SERVES 4

12 scallops
3 tbsp olive oil
350 g/12 oz dried
 conchiglie
150 ml/5 fl oz fish stock

1 onion, chopped
juice and finely grated
 rind of 2 lemons
150 ml/5 fl oz double
 cream

225 g/8 oz grated
 Cheddar cheese
salt and pepper
crusty brown bread,
 to serve

Baked Scallops with Pasta in Shells

Preheat the oven to 180°C/350°F/Gas Mark 4. Remove the scallops from their shells. Scrape off the skirt and the black intestinal thread. Reserve the white part (the flesh) and the orange part (the coral or roe). Very carefully ease the flesh and coral from the shell with a short, but very strong, knife. Wash the shells thoroughly and dry them well. Put the shells on a baking tray, sprinkle lightly with 2 tablespoons of the oil and set aside.

Meanwhile, bring a large saucepan of lightly salted water to the boil over a medium heat. Add the pasta and remaining oil and cook for 8–10 minutes, or until tender but still firm to the bite. Drain and divide the cooked pasta between the scallop shells.

Put the scallops, stock and onion in an ovenproof dish and season to taste with pepper. Cover with foil and bake in the preheated oven for 8 minutes.

Remove the dish from the oven. Remove the foil, then use a slotted spoon to transfer the scallops to the shells. Add 1 tablespoon of the cooking liquid to each shell, then sprinkle over a little lemon juice, lemon rind and cream, and top with the Cheddar cheese.

Increase the oven temperature to 230°C/450°F/Gas Mark 8 and return the scallops to the oven for a further 4 minutes.

Serve the scallops in their shells with crusty brown bread.

SERVES 6

450 g/1 lb raw prawns
25 g/1 oz butter
2 shallots, finely chopped
225 ml/8 fl oz dry white
    vermouth

350 ml/12 fl oz water
450 g/1 lb dried linguine
2 tbsp olive oil
450 g/1 lb prepared
    scallops, thawed if
    frozen

2 tbsp snipped fresh
    chives
salt and pepper

Linguine with Prawns & Scallops

Peel and devein the prawns, reserving the shells. Melt the butter in a heavy-based frying pan. Add the shallots and cook over a low heat, stirring occasionally, for 5 minutes, or until softened. Add the prawn shells and cook, stirring constantly, for 1 minute. Pour in the vermouth and cook, stirring, for 1 minute. Add the water, bring to the boil, then reduce the heat and simmer for 10 minutes, or until the liquid has reduced by half. Remove the frying pan from the heat.

Bring a large saucepan of lightly salted water to boil over a medium heat. Add the pasta, return to the boil and cook for 8–10 minutes, or until tender but still firm to the bite.

Meanwhile, heat the oil in a separate heavy-based frying pan. Add the scallops and prawns and cook, stirring frequently, for 2 minutes, or until the scallops are opaque and the prawns have changed colour. Strain the prawn-shell stock into the frying pan. Drain the pasta and add to the frying pan with the chives and season to taste with salt and pepper. Toss well over a low heat for 1 minute, then serve.

SERVES 6

1.25 kg/2 lb 12 oz live mussels, scrubbed and debearded
225 ml/8 fl oz dry white wine
2 large onions, chopped

115 g/4 oz unsalted butter
6 large garlic cloves, finely chopped
5 tbsp chopped fresh parsley

300 ml/10 fl oz double cream
400 g/14 oz dried conchiglie
salt and pepper

Conchiglie with Mussels

Discard any mussels with broken shells or any that refuse to close when tapped. Place the mussels in a large heavy-based saucepan, together with the wine and half of the onions. Cover and cook over a medium heat, shaking the saucepan frequently, for 2–3 minutes, or until the shells open. Remove the saucepan from the heat. Drain the mussels and reserve the cooking liquid. Discard any mussels that remain closed. Strain the cooking liquid through a muslin-lined sieve into a bowl and reserve.

Melt the butter in a saucepan. Add the remaining onions and cook until translucent. Stir in the garlic and cook for 1 minute. Gradually stir in the reserved cooking liquid. Stir in the parsley and cream and season to taste with salt and pepper. Bring to simmering point over a low heat.

Meanwhile, bring a large saucepan of lightly salted water to the boil over a medium heat. Add the pasta and cook for 8–10 minutes, or until tender but still firm to the bite. Drain and keep warm.

Reserve a few mussels for the garnish and remove the remainder from their shells. Stir the shelled mussels into the cream sauce and warm briefly. Transfer the pasta to a serving dish. Pour over the sauce and toss to coat. Garnish with the reserved mussels and serve.

SERVES 4

1 kg/2 lb 4 oz live clams, scrubbed
225 ml/8 fl oz dry white wine
2 garlic cloves, roughly chopped

4 tbsp chopped fresh flat-leaf parsley
2 tbsp olive oil
1 onion, chopped
8 plum tomatoes, peeled, deseeded and chopped

1 fresh red chilli, deseeded and chopped
350 g/12 oz dried linguine
salt and pepper

Linguine with Clams in Tomato Sauce

Discard any clams with broken shells or any that refuse to close when tapped. Pour the wine into a large heavy-based saucepan and add the garlic, half the parsley and the clams. Cover and cook over a high heat, shaking the saucepan occasionally, for 5 minutes, or until the shells have opened. Remove the clams with a slotted spoon, reserving the cooking liquid. Discard any that remain closed and remove half of the remainder from their shells. Keep the shelled and unshelled clams in separate covered bowls. Strain the cooking liquid through a muslin-lined sieve and reserve.

Heat the oil in a heavy-based saucepan. Add the onion and cook over a low heat for 5 minutes, or until softened. Add the tomatoes, chilli and reserved cooking liquid and season to taste with salt and pepper. Bring to the boil, partially cover the saucepan and simmer for 20 minutes.

Meanwhile, bring a large saucepan of lightly salted water to boil over a medium heat. Add the pasta, return to the boil and cook for 8–10 minutes, or until tender but still firm to the bite. Drain and transfer to a warmed serving dish.

Stir the shelled clams into the tomato sauce and heat through gently for 2–3 minutes. Pour over the pasta and toss. Garnish with the clams in their shells and remaining parsley. Serve immediately.

SERVES 4

5 tbsp lemon pepper oil, plus extra to serve
6 garlic cloves, crushed
675 g/1 lb 8 oz mixed seafood (prawns, squid, mussels)

dash of vodka
125 ml/4 fl oz white wine
1 sprig tarragon, leaves only
dash of salt

450 g/1 lb fettuccine
chopped flat-leaf parsley, to garnish

Fettuccine with Lemon Pepper Seafood

Heat a wok or deep frying pan and add the lemon pepper oil. When the oil is hot, add the garlic and seafood. Stir for 1 minute. Add a dash of vodka, the white wine, tarragon leaves and salt. Keep stirring until the seafood is cooked through.

Bring a large saucepan of lightly salted water to boil over a medium heat. Add the pasta and cook for 8–10 minutes, or until tender but still firm to the bite. Drain and add the pasta to the seafood mixture. Toss well and serve immediately on warmed plates. Drizzle more lemon pepper oil on top to serve and garnish with the chopped parsley.

SERVES 4

6 spring onions
350 g/12 oz crabmeat
2 tsp finely chopped fresh
  ginger
1/8–1/4 tsp chilli sauce or
  Tabasco sauce

700 g/1 lb 9 oz tomatoes,
  peeled, deseeded and
  roughly chopped
1 garlic clove, finely
  chopped
1 tbsp white wine vinegar
1 quantity Basic Pasta
  Dough (see p6)

plain flour, for dusting
1 egg, lightly beaten
2 tbsp double cream
salt
shredded spring onion,
  to garnish

Crab Ravioli

Thinly slice the spring onions, keeping the white and green parts separate. Mix the green spring onions, crabmeat, ginger and chilli sauce to taste together in a bowl. Cover and chill.

Place the tomatoes in a food processor and process to a purée. Place the garlic, white spring onions and vinegar in a saucepan and add the puréed tomatoes. Bring to the boil, then reduce the heat and simmer for 10 minutes. Remove from the heat and reserve.

Divide the pasta dough in half and wrap 1 piece in clingfilm. Roll out the other piece on a lightly floured surface to a rectangle 2–3 mm/1/16–1/8 inch thick. Cover with a damp tea towel and roll out the other piece of dough to the same size. Place small mounds, about 1 teaspoon each, of the filling in rows 4 cm/1½ inches apart on a sheet of pasta dough. Brush the spaces between the mounds with beaten egg. Lift the second sheet of dough on top of the first and press down firmly between the pockets of filling, pushing out any air bubbles. Using a pasta wheel or sharp knife, cut into squares. Place on a floured tea towel and leave to stand for 1 hour.

Bring a large saucepan of lightly salted water to the boil over a medium heat. Add the ravioli and cook for 5 minutes. Remove with a slotted spoon and drain on kitchen paper. Gently heat the tomato sauce and whisk in the cream. Place the ravioli on serving plates, pour over the sauce, garnish with shredded spring onion and serve.

Vegetarian

SERVES 4

600 ml/1 pint milk
1 onion, peeled
8 peppercorns
1 bay leaf
55 g/2 oz butter
40 g/1½ oz plain flour

½ tsp ground nutmeg
5 tbsp double cream
pepper
100 g/3½ oz mature
   Cheddar cheese,
   grated

100 g/3½ oz Roquefort
   cheese, crumbled
350 g/12 oz dried
   macaroni
100 g/3½ oz Gruyère
   or Emmental cheese,
   grated

Macaroni Cheese

Put the milk, onion, peppercorns and bay leaf in a pan and bring to the boil. Remove from the heat and let stand for 15 minutes.

Melt the butter in a pan and stir in the flour until well combined and smooth. Cook over a medium heat, stirring constantly, for 1 minute. Remove from the heat. Strain the milk to remove the solids and stir a little into the butter and flour mixture until well incorporated. Return to the heat and gradually add the remaining milk, stirring constantly, until it has all been incorporated. Cook for a further 3 minutes, or until the sauce is smooth and thickened, then add the nutmeg, cream and season to taste with pepper. Add the Cheddar and Roquefort cheeses and stir until melted.

Meanwhile, bring a large saucepan of lightly salted water to boil over a medium heat. Add the macaroni, then return to the boil and cook for 8–10 minutes, or until just tender. Drain well and add to the cheese sauce. Stir well together.

Preheat the grill to high. Spoon the mixture into an ovenproof serving dish, then scatter over the Gruyère cheese and cook under the grill until bubbling and brown. Serve immediately.

SERVES 4

3 tbsp olive oil
4 courgettes, halved lengthways and thickly sliced
3 red peppers, deseeded and chopped
1 aubergine, chopped
2 red onions, chopped

5 shallots, peeled and quartered
250 g/9 oz button mushrooms
400 g/14 oz canned chopped tomatoes
1 tbsp tomato purée
50 g/1¾ oz butter

50 g/1¾ oz plain flour
600 ml/1 pint milk
100 g/3½ oz Cheddar cheese, grated
200 g/7 oz fresh lasagne
2 tbsp grated Parmesan cheese
salt and pepper

Roast Vegetable Lasagne

Preheat the oven to 190°C/375°F/Gas Mark 5. Put the oil in a large bowl, add the courgettes, peppers, aubergine, onions and shallots and toss well to coat. Divide the vegetables between 2 baking trays and roast in the preheated oven for 30–40 minutes until soft and flecked with brown. Add the button mushrooms after 20 minutes. Remove the vegetables from the oven and tip into a large bowl. Add the tomatoes and tomato purée and mix well.

Melt the butter in a saucepan over a low heat. Stir in the flour and cook, stirring constantly, for 2–3 minutes. Gradually add the milk and cook, continuing to stir constantly, until the sauce is thick and smooth. Season to taste with salt and pepper and stir in the Cheddar cheese.

Layer the vegetable mixture and sauce in an ovenproof dish with the lasagne, finishing with a layer of sauce. Sprinkle over the Parmesan cheese and bake in the oven for 30–35 minutes. Remove from the oven and serve hot.

SERVES 4

4 garlic cloves
500 g/1 lb 2 oz pumpkin,
  peeled, deseeded and
  cut into large chunks

4 sun-dried tomatoes in
  oil, drained, plus 2 tbsp
  oil from the jar
115 g/4 oz ricotta cheese
1 tbsp finely chopped
  fresh rosemary

1 quantity Basic Pasta
  Dough (see p6)
plain flour, for dusting
1 egg, lightly beaten
salt and pepper

Pumpkin + Ricotta Ravioli

Preheat the oven to 200°C/400°F/Gas Mark 6. Place the unpeeled garlic cloves on a baking sheet and bake for 10 minutes. Meanwhile, put the pumpkin in a steamer set over a pan of boiling water. Cover and steam for 15 minutes, until tender.

Chop the sun-dried tomatoes. Squeeze the garlic cloves out of their skins into a bowl. Add the pumpkin, sun-dried tomatoes, ricotta and rosemary and mash well with a potato masher until thoroughly combined. Season to taste with salt and pepper and leave to cool.

Divide the pasta dough in half and wrap 1 piece in clingfilm. Roll out the other piece on a lightly floured surface to a rectangle 2–3 mm/1/16–1/8 inch thick. Cover with a damp tea towel and roll out the other piece of dough to the same size. Place small mounds, about 1 teaspoon each, of the pumpkin filling in rows 4 cm/1½ inches apart on a sheet of pasta dough. Brush the spaces between the mounds with beaten egg. Lift the second sheet of dough on top and press down firmly between the pockets of filling, pushing out any air bubbles. Using a pasta wheel or sharp knife, cut into squares. Place on a floured tea towel and leave to stand for 1 hour.

Bring a large saucepan of lightly salted water to boil over a medium heat. Add the ravioli, bring back to the boil and cook for 3–4 minutes, until tender. Drain, toss with the oil from the sun-dried tomatoes and serve immediately.

SERVES 4

2 large aubergines
3 large courgettes
6 large tomatoes
1 large green pepper
1 large red pepper
3 garlic cloves

1 large onion
125 ml/4 fl oz olive oil
4½ tsp tomato purée
½ tsp chopped fresh
  basil, plus extra sprigs
  to garnish
1 quantity Basic Pasta
  Dough (see p6)

plain flour, for dusting
6 tbsp butter
150 ml/5 fl oz single
  cream
85 g/3 oz freshly grated
  Parmesan cheese
salt and pepper

Vegetable Ravioli

To make the filling, cut the aubergines and the courgettes into 2.5-cm/1-inch chunks. Place the aubergine pieces in a colander, sprinkle with salt and leave for about 20 minutes. Rinse and drain, then pat dry on kitchen paper.

Blanch the tomatoes in boiling water for 2 minutes. Drain, peel and chop the flesh. Core and deseed the peppers and cut into 2.5-cm/1-inch dice. Chop the garlic and onion. Heat the oil in a large pan over a low heat. Add the garlic and onion and cook for 3 minutes. Stir in the aubergines, courgettes, tomatoes, peppers, tomato purée and chopped basil. Season to taste with salt and pepper, cover and simmer for 20 minutes.

Roll out the pasta dough on a lightly floured surface to a rectangle 2–3 mm/$\frac{1}{16}$–$\frac{1}{8}$ inch thick. Using a 5-cm/2-inch plain biscuit cutter, stamp out rounds. Place small mounds, about 1 teaspoon each, of the filling on half of the rounds. Brush the edges with a little water, then cover with the remaining rounds, pressing the edges to seal. Place on a floured tea towel and leave to stand for 1 hour. Preheat the oven to 200°C/400°F/Gas Mark 6.

Bring a large saucepan of lightly salted water to the boil over a medium heat. Add the ravioli and cook for about 3–4 minutes. Drain and transfer to a greased ovenproof dish, dotting each layer with butter. Pour over the cream and sprinkle over the Parmesan cheese. Bake in the preheated oven for 20 minutes. Garnish with basil sprigs and serve immediately.

SERVES 4

450 g/1 lb dried
spaghetti
175 g/6 oz unsalted
butter

4 tbsp chopped fresh
flat-leaf parsley, plus
extra for garnishing

225 g/8 oz Parmesan
cheese, grated
salt and pepper

Spaghetti with Parsley + Parmesan

Bring a large saucepan of lightly salted water to boil over a medium heat. Add the pasta, bring back to the boil and cook for 8–10 minutes, or until tender but firm to the bite. Drain and tip into a warmed serving dish.

Add the butter, parsley and half the Parmesan cheese and toss well, using 2 forks, until the butter and cheese have melted. Season to taste with salt and pepper and serve immediately sprinkled with the remaining Parmesan cheese.

SERVES 4

225 g/8 oz dried fusilli
1 head broccoli, cut into florets
2 courgettes, sliced
225 g/8 oz asparagus spears, trimmed
125 g/4½ oz mangetout

125 g/4½ oz frozen peas
25 g/1 oz butter
3 tbsp vegetable stock
5 tbsp double cream
large pinch of freshly grated nutmeg

2 tbsp chopped fresh parsley
salt and pepper
2 tbsp freshly grated Parmesan cheese, to serve

Pasta with Green Vegetables

Bring a large saucepan of lightly salted water to boil over a medium heat. Add the pasta, return to the boil and cook for 8–10 minutes, or until tender but still firm to the bite. Drain well and return to the saucepan, cover and keep warm.

Steam the broccoli, courgettes, asparagus spears and mangetout over a saucepan of boiling, salted water until just beginning to soften. Remove from the heat and plunge into cold water to prevent further cooking. Drain and reserve. Cook the peas in boiling, salted water for 3 minutes, then drain. Refresh in cold water and drain again.

Place the butter and stock in a saucepan over a medium heat. Add all the vegetables except for the asparagus spears and toss carefully with a wooden spoon to heat through, taking care not to break them up. Stir in the cream, allow the sauce to heat through and season to taste with salt, pepper and nutmeg.

Transfer the pasta to a warmed serving dish and stir in the chopped parsley. Spoon the sauce over and arrange the asparagus spears on top. Sprinkle with the freshly grated Parmesan cheese and serve hot.

SERVES 4

12 dried cannelloni tubes
1 aubergine
125 ml/4 fl oz olive oil,
    plus extra for brushing
225 g/8 oz spinach
2 garlic cloves, crushed
1 tsp ground cumin

85 g/3 oz mushrooms,
    chopped
55 g/2 oz mozzarella
    cheese, sliced
salt and pepper
lamb's lettuce, to garnish

tomato sauce

1 tbsp olive oil
1 onion, chopped
2 garlic cloves, crushed
800 g/1 lb 12 oz canned
    chopped tomatoes
1 tsp caster sugar
2 tbsp chopped fresh
    basil

Vegetable Cannelloni

Preheat the oven to 190°C/375°F/Gas Mark 5. Bring a large saucepan of lightly salted water to boil over a medium heat. Add the cannelloni tubes, return to the boil and cook for 8–10 minutes, or until tender but still firm to the bite. Transfer the pasta to a plate and pat dry with kitchen paper. Brush a large ovenproof dish with oil.

Cut the aubergine into small dice. Heat the oil in a frying pan over a medium heat. Add the aubergine and cook, stirring frequently, for about 2–3 minutes.

Add the spinach, garlic, cumin and mushrooms and reduce the heat. Season to taste with salt and pepper and cook, stirring, for about 2–3 minutes. Spoon the mixture into the cannelloni tubes and put into the dish in a single layer.

To make the sauce, heat the oil in a pan over a medium heat. Add the onion and garlic and cook for 1 minute. Add the tomatoes, sugar and basil and bring to the boil. Reduce the heat and simmer for about 5 minutes. Spoon the sauce over the cannelloni tubes.

Arrange the mozzarella cheese on top of the sauce and bake in the preheated oven for about 30 minutes, or until the cheese is golden brown and bubbling. Serve garnished with lamb's lettuce.

SERVES 4

12 dried cannelloni tubes
6 tbsp olive oil, plus extra
  for brushing
1 onion, finely chopped
2 garlic cloves, finely
  chopped
800 g/1 lb 12 oz canned
  chopped tomatoes
1 tbsp tomato purée

8 black olives, stoned
  and chopped
25 g/1 oz butter
450 g/1 lb wild
  mushrooms, finely
  chopped
85 g/3 oz fresh
  breadcrumbs
150 ml/5 fl oz milk

225 g/8 oz ricotta cheese
6 tbsp freshly grated
  Parmesan cheese
2 tbsp pine kernels
2 tbsp flaked almonds
salt and pepper

Mushroom Cannelloni

Preheat the oven to 190°C/375°F/Gas Mark 5. Bring a large saucepan of lightly
salted water to boil over a medium heat. Add the cannelloni tubes, return to the
boil and cook for 8–10 minutes, or until tender but still firm to the bite. With a slotted
spoon, transfer the cannelloni tubes to a plate and pat dry. Brush a large ovenproof
dish with oil.

Heat 2 tablespoons of the oil in a frying pan, add the onion and half the garlic and
cook over a low heat for 5 minutes, or until softened. Add the tomatoes and their
can juices, tomato purée and olives and season to taste with salt and pepper. Bring
to the boil and cook for 3–4 minutes. Pour the sauce into the ovenproof dish.

To make the filling, melt the butter in a heavy-based frying pan. Add the
mushrooms and remaining garlic and cook over a medium heat, stirring frequently,
for 3–5 minutes, or until tender. Remove the frying pan from the heat. Mix the
breadcrumbs, milk and remaining oil together in a large bowl, then stir in the ricotta,
the mushroom mixture and 4 tablespoons of the Parmesan cheese. Season to taste
with salt and pepper.

Fill the cannelloni tubes with the mushroom mixture and place them in the
prepared dish. Brush with oil and sprinkle with the remaining Parmesan cheese,
the pine kernels and almonds. Bake in the preheated oven for 25 minutes, or until
golden. Serve immediately.

SERVES 4

450 g/1 lb dried spaghetti
125 ml/4 fl oz extra virgin olive oil

3 garlic cloves, finely chopped
3 tbsp chopped fresh flat-leaf parsley

salt and pepper

Spaghetti Olio E Aglio

Bring a large saucepan of lightly salted water to boil over a medium heat. Add the pasta, return to the boil and cook for 8–10 minutes, or until tender but still firm to the bite.

Meanwhile, heat the oil in a heavy-based frying pan. Add the garlic and a pinch of salt and cook over a low heat, stirring constantly, for 3–4 minutes, or until golden. Do not allow the garlic to brown or it will taste bitter. Remove the frying pan from the heat.

Drain the pasta and transfer to a warmed serving dish. Pour in the garlic-flavoured oil, then add the chopped parsley and season to taste with salt and pepper. Toss well and serve immediately.

SERVES 4

400 g/14 oz dried rigatoni
25 g/1 oz unsalted butter
6 fresh sage leaves

200 g/7 oz Gorgonzola
cheese, diced
175–225 ml/6–8 fl oz
double cream

2 tbsp dry vermouth
salt and pepper

Rigatoni with Gorgonzola Sauce

Bring a large saucepan of lightly salted water to boil over a medium heat. Add the pasta, return to the boil and cook for 8–10 minutes, until tender but still firm to the bite.

Meanwhile, melt the butter in a separate heavy-based saucepan. Add the sage leaves and cook, stirring gently, for 1 minute. Remove and reserve the sage leaves. Add the cheese and cook, stirring constantly, over a low heat until it has melted. Gradually, stir in 175 ml/6 fl oz of the cream and the vermouth. Season to taste with salt and pepper and cook, stirring, until thickened. Add more cream if the sauce seems too thick.

Drain the pasta well and transfer to a warmed serving dish. Add the Gorgonzola sauce, toss well to mix and serve immediately, garnished with the reserved sage leaves.

SERVES 4

225 g/8 oz dried haricot beans, soaked overnight and drained
225 g/8 oz dried penne
6 tbsp olive oil
850 ml/1½ pints vegetable stock
2 large onions, sliced
2 garlic cloves, chopped
2 bay leaves
1 tsp dried oregano
1 tsp dried thyme
5 tbsp red wine
2 tbsp tomato purée
2 celery sticks, sliced
1 fennel bulb, sliced
115 g/4 oz mushrooms, sliced
225 g/8 oz tomatoes, sliced
1 tsp dark muscovado sugar
55 g/2 oz dry white breadcrumbs
salt and pepper
crusty bread, to serve

Pasta + Bean Casserole

Preheat the oven to 180°C/350°F/Gas Mark 4. Put the beans in a large pan, add water to cover and bring to the boil. Boil the beans rapidly for 20 minutes, then drain them and set aside.

Bring a large saucepan of lightly salted water to the boil over a medium heat. Add the pasta, return to the boil and cook for 3 minutes, adding 1 tablespoon of the oil. Drain in a colander and set aside.

Put the beans in a large flameproof casserole, pour in the stock and stir in the remaining oil, the onions, garlic, bay leaves, herbs, wine and tomato purée. Bring to the boil, cover the casserole and cook in the preheated oven for 2 hours.

Remove the casserole from the oven and add the reserved pasta, the celery, fennel, mushrooms and tomatoes and season to taste with salt and pepper. Stir in the sugar and sprinkle the breadcrumbs on top. Cover the casserole again, return to the oven and continue cooking for 1 hour. Serve with crusty bread.

SERVES 4

140 g/5 oz fontina cheese, thinly sliced
300 ml/10 fl oz béchamel sauce

6 tbsp butter, plus extra for greasing
350 g/12 oz mixed wild mushrooms, sliced
350 g/12 oz dried tagliatelle

2 egg yolks
4 tbsp freshly grated Romano cheese
salt and pepper

Baked Pasta with Mushrooms

Stir the fontina cheese into the béchamel sauce and set aside.

Melt 2 tablespoons of the butter in a large saucepan. Add the mushrooms and cook over low heat, stirring occasionally, for 10 minutes.

Meanwhile, bring a large saucepan of lightly salted water to boil over a medium heat. Add the pasta, return to the boil and cook for 8–10 minutes, or until tender but still firm to the bite. Drain, return to the pan and add the remaining butter, the egg yolks and about one third of the sauce, then season with salt and pepper. Toss well to mix, then gently stir in the mushrooms.

Lightly grease a large, ovenproof dish with butter and spoon in the pasta mixture. Pour over the remaining sauce evenly and sprinkle with the grated Romano cheese. Bake in a preheated oven, 200°C/400°F/Gas Mark 6, for 15–20 minutes, or until golden brown. Spoon out into serving bowls and serve immediately.

SERVES 4

300 g/10½ oz dried penne or pasta shape of your choice
2 tbsp olive oil
250 g/9 oz mushrooms, sliced

1 tsp dried oregano
250 ml/9 fl oz vegetable stock
1 tbsp lemon juice
6 tbsp cream cheese

200 g/7 oz frozen spinach leaves
salt and pepper

Creamy Spinach & Mushroom Pasta

Bring a large saucepan of lightly salted water to boil over a medium heat. Add the pasta, bring back to the boil and cook for 8–10 minutes, or until tender but firm to the bite. Drain, reserving 175 ml/6 fl oz of the cooking liquid.

Meanwhile, heat the oil in a large, heavy-based frying pan over a medium heat, add the mushrooms and cook, stirring frequently, for 8 minutes, or until almost crisp. Stir in the oregano, stock and lemon juice and cook for 10–12 minutes, or until the sauce is reduced by half.

Stir in the cream cheese and spinach and cook over a medium–low heat for 3–5 minutes. Add the reserved cooking liquid, then the cooked pasta. Stir well, season to taste with salt and pepper and heat through before serving immediately.

SERVES 4

2 tbsp olive oil
2 yellow peppers,
  deseeded and
  chopped
1 mild onion, finely
  chopped
1 small aubergine,
  chopped

400 g/14 oz canned
  chopped tomatoes
  with herbs
1 tbsp tomato purée
2 tbsp hot water, plus
  extra if needed
250 g/9 oz dried
  wholewheat pasta
  spirals

100 g/3½ oz Cheddar
  cheese, grated
40 g/1½ oz slightly stale
  wholemeal or white
  breadcrumbs
salt and pepper

Cheesy Pasta Casserole

Heat the oil in a large, non-stick frying pan over a medium heat, add the yellow peppers, onion and aubergine and cook, stirring occasionally, for 15 minutes, or until soft.

Add the tomatoes and their juice, tomato purée, hot water to the frying pan, season to taste with salt and pepper and stir well. Bring to a simmer and cook for 15 minutes. Stir in a little more water if the mixture is not fairly sloppy. Preheat the oven to 190°C/375°F/Gas Mark 5.

Bring a large saucepan of lightly salted water to the boil over a medium heat. Add the pasta and cook for 8–10 minutes, or until tender but still firm to the bite. Drain and tip into a suitably sized, shallow ovenproof dish. Add the tomato mixture and mix together well. Spread out evenly in the dish.

Mix the Cheddar cheese and breadcrumbs together, then sprinkle evenly over the pasta mixture. Bake in the preheated oven for 20–25 minutes until the top is golden. Serve immediately.

SERVES 4

2 tbsp olive oil
1 tbsp butter
1 small onion, finely
  chopped
4 peppers, yellow and
  red, deseeded and
  cut into 2-cm/¾-inch
  squares

3 garlic cloves, thinly
  sliced
450 g/1 lb dried rigatoni
125 g/4½ oz goat's
  cheese, crumbled

15 fresh basil leaves,
  shredded
10 black olives, stoned
  and sliced
salt and pepper

Rigatoni with Peppers & Goat's Cheese

Heat the oil and butter in a large frying pan over a medium heat. Add the onion and cook until soft. Raise the heat to medium–high and add the peppers and garlic. Cook for 12–15 minutes, stirring, until the peppers are tender but not mushy. Season to taste with salt and pepper. Remove from the heat.

Bring a large saucepan of lightly salted water to the boil over medium heat. Add the pasta, bring back to the boil and cook for 8–10 minutes, or until tender but still firm to the bite. Drain and transfer to a warmed serving dish. Add the goat's cheese and toss to mix.

Briefly reheat the onion and pepper mixture. Add the basil and olives. Pour over the pasta and toss well to mix. Serve immediately.

SERVES 2–4

350 g/12 oz fresh pasta shapes
½ tsp salt
6 tbsp olive oil

½ tsp freshly grated nutmeg
½ tsp black pepper
1 garlic clove, crushed
2 tbsp tapenade

85g/3 oz black or green olives, stoned and sliced
1 tbsp chopped fresh parsley, to garnish (optional)

Pasta with Spicy Olive Sauce

Bring a large saucepan of lightly salted water to boil over a medium heat. Add the pasta, bring back to the boil and cook for 8–10 minutes, or until tender but firm to the bite.

Meanwhile, put the ½ teaspoon of salt with the oil, nutmeg, pepper, garlic, tapenade and olives in another saucepan and heat slowly but don't allow to boil. Cover and leave to stand for 3–4 minutes.

Drain the pasta and return to the saucepan. Add the flavoured oil and heat gently for 1–2 minutes. Serve immediately garnished with chopped parsley, if using.

SERVES 4

350 g/12 oz dried
  vermicelli
3 courgettes
3 carrots
25 g/1 oz unsalted butter
1 tbsp olive oil

2 garlic cloves, finely
  chopped
85 g/3 oz fresh basil,
  shredded
25 g/1 oz fresh chives,
  finely snipped

25 g/1 oz fresh flat-leaf
  parsley, finely chopped
1 small head radicchio,
  leaves shredded
salt and pepper

Vermicelli with Vegetable Ribbons

Bring a large saucepan of lightly salted water to boil over a medium heat. Add the pasta, return to the boil and cook for 5 minutes, or until tender but still firm to the bite.

Meanwhile, cut the courgettes and carrots into very thin strips with a swivel-blade vegetable peeler or a mandolin. Melt the butter with the oil in a heavy-based frying pan. Add the carrot strips and garlic and cook over a low heat, stirring occasionally, for 5 minutes. Add the courgette strips and all the herbs and season to taste with salt and pepper.

Drain the pasta and add it to the frying pan. Toss well to mix and cook, stirring occasionally, for 5 minutes. Transfer to a warmed serving dish, add the radicchio, toss well and serve immediately.

SERVES 4

6 tbsp olive oil
1 small onion, very thinly sliced
2 garlic cloves, very finely chopped
2 tbsp chopped fresh rosemary

1 tbsp chopped fresh flat-leaf parsley
450 g/1 lb small courgettes, cut into 4-cm/1½-inch strips
finely grated rind of 1 lemon

450 g/1 lb dried fusilli
salt and pepper
4 tbsp freshly grated Parmesan cheese, to serve

Fusilli with Courgette & Lemon

Heat the oil in a large frying pan over a medium–low heat. Add the onion and cook gently, stirring occasionally, for about 10 minutes, until golden.

Raise the heat to medium–high. Add the garlic, rosemary and parsley. Cook for a few seconds, stirring.

Add the courgettes and lemon rind. Cook for 5–7 minutes, stirring occasionally, until the courgettes are just tender. Season to taste with salt and pepper. Remove from the heat.

Bring a large saucepan of lightly salted water to the boil over a medium heat. Add the pasta, bring back to the boil and cook for 8–10 minutes, or until tender but still firm to the bite. Drain and transfer to a warmed serving dish.

Briefly reheat the courgette sauce. Pour over the pasta and toss well to mix. Sprinkle with the Parmesan cheese and serve immediately.

SERVES 4

100 ml/3½ fl oz olive oil
1 onion, finely chopped
200 g/7 oz black olives, stoned and roughly chopped

400 g/14 oz canned chopped tomatoes, drained
2 red, yellow or orange peppers, deseeded and cut into thin strips

350 g/12 oz dried fettuccine
salt and pepper
freshly grated pecorino cheese, to serve

Fettuccine with Peppers + Olives

Heat the oil in a large, heavy-based saucepan. Add the onion and cook over a low heat, stirring occasionally, for 5 minutes, or until softened. Add the olives, tomatoes and peppers and season to taste with salt and pepper. Cover and simmer gently over a very low heat, stirring occasionally, for 35 minutes.

Meanwhile, bring a large saucepan of lightly salted water to boil over a medium heat. Add the pasta, return to the boil and cook for 8–10 minutes, or until tender but still firm to the bite. Drain the pasta and transfer to a warmed serving dish.

Spoon the sauce onto the pasta and toss well. Sprinkle generously with the pecorino cheese and serve immediately.

SERVES 4

2 garlic cloves
85 g/3 oz hazelnuts
140 g/5 oz rocket, coarse
  stalks removed

115 g/4 oz freshly grated
  Parmesan cheese, plus
  extra to serve
6 tbsp extra virgin olive oil

115 g/4 oz mascarpone
  cheese
400 g/14 oz dried
  spaghetti
salt and pepper

Spaghetti with Rocket & Hazelnut Pesto

Put the garlic and hazelnuts in a food processor and process until finely chopped. Add the rocket, Parmesan cheese and oil and process until smooth and thoroughly combined. Scrape the pesto into a serving dish, season to taste with salt and pepper and stir in the mascarpone cheese.

Bring a large saucepan of lightly salted water to the boil over medium heat. Add the pasta, bring back to the boil and cook for 8–10 minutes, until tender but still firm to the bite.

Stir 100–150 ml/3½–5 fl oz of the pasta cooking water into the pesto, mixing well until thoroughly combined. Drain the pasta, add to the bowl and toss well to coat. Sprinkle with more Parmesan cheese and serve immediately.

SERVES 4

1 onion, chopped
400 g/14 oz canned
  chopped tomatoes
225 ml/8 fl oz milk
1–2 red chillies, deseeded
  and finely chopped

1 garlic clove, finely
  chopped
pinch of ground
  coriander
280 g/10 oz dried
  conchiglie

85 g/3 oz Gruyère
  cheese, grated
salt and pepper

Hot Tomato & Conchiglie Gratin

Put the onion, tomatoes and milk in a large heavy-based saucepan and bring just to the boil. Add the chillies, garlic, coriander and pasta, season to taste with salt and pepper and cook over a medium heat, stirring frequently, for 2–3 minutes.

Add just enough water to cover and cook, stirring frequently, for 8–10 minutes, or until the pasta is tender but still firm to the bite. Meanwhile, preheat the grill.

Spoon the pasta mixture into individual flameproof dishes and sprinkle evenly with the cheese. Place under the grill for 3–4 minutes, until the cheese has melted. Serve immediately.

SERVES 4

1 red pepper
1 orange pepper
280 g/10 oz dried
   conchiglie

5 tbsp extra virgin olive oil
2 tbsp lemon juice
2 tbsp pesto
1 garlic clove, crushed

3 tbsp shredded fresh
   basil leaves
salt and pepper

Pasta Salad with Chargrilled Peppers

Put the whole peppers on a baking sheet and place under a preheated grill, turning frequently, for 15 minutes, until charred all over. Remove with tongs and place in a bowl. Cover with crumpled kitchen paper and set aside.

Meanwhile, bring a large saucepan of lightly salted water to boil over a medium heat. Add the pasta, bring back to the boil and cook for 8–10 minutes, until tender but still firm to the bite.

Combine the oil, lemon juice, pesto and garlic in a bowl, whisking well to mix. Drain the pasta, add it to the pesto mixture while still hot and toss well. Set aside.

When the peppers are cool enough to handle, peel off the skins, then cut open and remove the seeds. Chop the flesh roughly and add to the pasta with the basil. Season to taste with salt and pepper and toss well. Serve at room temperature.

SERVES 4

butter, for greasing
250 g/9 oz fusilli
450 g/1 lb purple
  sprouting broccoli
6 tbsp olive oil, plus extra
  for drizzling

2 shallots, thinly sliced
1 fresh red chilli,
  deseeded and finely
  chopped
2 garlic cloves, finely
  chopped

70 g/2½ oz coarse fresh
  breadcrumbs
  (from a ciabatta loaf)
55 g/2 oz roughly grated
  Parmesan cheese
salt and pepper

Pasta + Broccoli Gratin

Preheat the oven to 200°C/400°F/Gas Mark 6. Butter a high-sided 2.5-litre/4½-pint baking dish. Bring a pan of lightly salted water to the boil over a medium heat. Add the pasta and cook for 8–10 minutes, or until tender but still firm to the bite. Drain thoroughly and tip into the baking dish.

Meanwhile, put the broccoli florets, leaves and stems in a steamer basket set over boiling water. Steam for 4 minutes until only just tender. Remove from the heat and set aside, reserving the water in the pan.

Heat a frying pan over medium–low heat. Add the oil and gently fry the shallots, chilli and garlic for 5 minutes until soft and just starting to colour.

Add the broccoli and 150 ml/5 fl oz of the broccoli cooking water to the dish. Season to taste with salt and pepper and toss to mix. Add the shallot mixture and the oil from the pan. Toss again to mix.

Scatter the breadcrumbs over the top, then sprinkle with the Parmesan and a little more salt and pepper. Drizzle the crumbs with more oil. Bake in the oven for 15–20 minutes until golden and crisp.

SERVES 4

4 plum tomatoes, peeled, deseeded and chopped

4 garlic cloves, finely chopped

8 black olives, stoned and finely chopped

1 fresh red chilli, deseeded and finely chopped

2 tbsp chopped fresh flat-leaf parsley

2 tbsp extra virgin olive oil

1 tbsp lemon juice

280 g/10 oz dried fettuccine

salt and pepper

Fettuccine with Garlic, Tomatoes + Olives

Place the tomatoes in a large, non-metallic sieve set over a bowl. Cover and set aside in the refrigerator for 30 minutes.

Combine the garlic, olives, chilli, parsley, oil and lemon juice in a separate bowl. Season to taste with salt and pepper. Cover and set aside in the refrigerator until required. Add the tomatoes to the garlic mixture, discarding the drained juice.

Bring a large saucepan of lightly salted water to the boil over a medium heat. Add the fettuccine, return to the boil and cook for 8–10 minutes, or until tender but still firm to the bite. Drain, then tip into a serving bowl. Add the garlic and tomato mixture and toss well. Serve immediately.

SERVES 4–6

2 aubergines, sliced crossways into 2-cm/¾-inch slices
olive oil for brushing
55 g/2 oz butter, plus extra for greasing
1 onion, chopped

2 large garlic cloves, finely chopped
½ tsp dried oregano
2 small strips lemon peel
650 g/1 lb 7 oz canned chopped tomatoes and juice

280 g/10 oz penne
1 egg, lightly beaten
250 g/9 oz grated mozzarella cheese
25 g/1 oz Parmesan cheese shavings
salt and pepper

Penne with Aubergines & Tomato Sauce

Arrange the aubergines in a single layer on a roasting tray. Brush with olive oil on both sides and place under a very hot grill. Grill for 10–12 minutes, turning once, until lightly coloured. Transfer to a plate, season with salt and pepper and keep warm.

Heat the butter in a frying pan over medium heat. Add the onion and gently fry for 7 minutes until starting to colour. Add the garlic, oregano and lemon peel, and fry for another 2 minutes. Stir in the tomatoes, and season to taste with salt and pepper. Bring to the boil, then reduce the heat and simmer for 5–7 minutes until slightly reduced.

Meanwhile, bring a large saucepan of lightly salted water to the boil over a medium heat. Add the pasta and cook for 8–10 minutes, or until tender but still firm to the bite. Drain, return to the pan and stir in the beaten egg. Preheat the oven to 200°C/400°F/Gas Mark 6. Butter a high-sided 2.5-litre/4½-pint baking dish.

Tip half the penne into the base of the dish. Arrange the aubergine slices in a single layer on top, and sprinkle with half the mozzarella cheese. Pour the tomato sauce over the aubergines, followed by the remaining penne. Sprinkle with the remaining mozzarella cheese and scatter the Parmesan shavings over the top. Bake in the oven for 20 minutes until the top is golden and crisp.